Dare to Live

Reflections on fear, courage

and wholeness

First published by O-Books, 2008
Reprinted 2010
O-Books is an imprint of John Hunt Publishing Ltd., Laurel House, Station Approach,
Alresford, Hants, SO24 9JH, UK
office1@o-books.net
www.o-books.com

For distributor details and how to order please visit the 'Ordering' section on our website.

Text copyright: Miriam Subirana 2008

Original title: Atreverse a vivr. Reflexiones sobre
el miedo, la valentia y la plenitud.
Published by RBA, Barcelona, Spain 2007.
Translation Caroline Wilson
Cover illustration by Miriam Subirana: It is
possible to dream III
www.miriamsubirana.com

ISBN: 978 1 84694 120 7

A CIP catalogue record for this book is available from the British Library.

Design: Stuart Davies

Printed in the UK by CPI Antony Rowe
Printed in the USA by Offset Paperback Mfrs, Inc

We operate a distinctive and ethical publishing philosophy in all
areas of our business, from our global network of authors to
production and worldwide distribution.

Dare to Live

*Reflections on fear, courage
and wholeness*

Miriam Subirana

BKIS

BOOKS

Winchester, UK
Washington, USA

DEDICATION

This book is dedicated to

Those who are tired of living under the shadow of fear and are ready to awaken and stop creating their own suffering.

Those who know that their fears are defences, insecurities and blockages, and wish to live with greater authenticity, transparency and light.

Those who know that not all is as it seems and want to see behind appearances.

Those who dare to go into the depths of their being in order to emerge with all their beauty and shine with all their strengths.

Those who wish to achieve happiness and wholeness in their life.

The Comforter of hearts, That One who gives us light and wisdom in order to create a destiny of happiness and hope.

The Brahma Kumaris World Spiritual University, for teaching the deepest education that exists for the care of the soul.

As they didn't know it was impossible, they did it.

CONTENTS

PROLOGUE

THE CHALLENGE

I will read this book at least once more, I said to myself, at about page one hundred, and when I reached the end, I started again.

The fact is, that in it, Miriam Subirana describes us. It is a mirror book. I doubt that there is anybody who does not feel portrayed in some of her observations, unadorned, without justifications, without moral judgement.

It is about fears and their offspring: doubts, mistrust, insecurity; about fears and their multiple causes. Because very often we are not able to identify our fears, the author shows us how they are expressed in us, in the form of worries, anxiety, anguish, tension and anger. Fear is one of the things that is most responsible for human behaviour, for our relationships and the functioning of the world. Fear blocks, separates, isolates and puts us in opposition. To dilute it is alchemy, it is transformation, and there is only one path: from the inside out. This book is talking about daily life and how to live it better, and does so with depth and concision. We are all creators, and our thoughts, emotions and attitudes are our own creation; therein lies freedom, inseparable from responsibility.

Jagdish Chander, a Raj Yogui teacher from India, told Miriam Subirana a personal anecdote. He was in New York when one night his way was blocked by a group of three or four men threatening him. He asked them if they knew the typical dance from India and he started to dance. The men smiled; and Jagdish went off down the street dancing.

This kind of answer can only be given by a person who is sure of themselves, who is not afraid and who doesn't have their creativity blocked off.

Courage is a human quality, not a gift belonging to a few. It must be made to flower, it must be worked at. We should know what we carry within, the potential and the learnt fears. This book is a path, a serious proposal of reflection and change, but it does not seek to deceive anybody, the effort involved is great. The author suggests to us a first act of courage: accepting the challenge. And to do so she establishes a relationship with classical philosophy, 'know yourself'. As she says: "In order to know yourself you need time, silence, introspection, discipline, observation, knowledge and meditation".

The three fundamental values that she highlights in order to begin on this path are: courage, trust and tolerance, and she offers valuable and original ideas with which to cultivate them. She says courage, for example, is strengthened by cultivating curiosity. That to trust is to accept one's own freedom and that of others, being open to ideas. And she makes it clear to us that to tolerate does not mean to put up with. To tolerate is to accept, understand and know how to confront. In tolerance you dissolve that which, otherwise, you would be putting up with.

A practical piece of advice: expanding obstacles and problems in your mind (letting them go round and round in your head), or talking to others about them, means to create mountains. Don't expand problems. Put a full stop and turn the page, and that way you will go forward. Expansion is the longest way towards understanding, it consumes your time and energy, and to go to what is essential is a short-cut. That is being tolerant.

In the West, Miriam Subirana tells us, we have the inner belief that love, worry, fear and suffering go together. She quotes a delightful line from Eleanor Roosevelt: "No one can hurt you without your consent". Let's look again at our beliefs.

We do not live in isolation, relationships form us, and we have learned the majority of beliefs that constitute our actions.

We live under the illusion that we can take happiness from objects, people and places. But happiness is what we feel when we put our heart into something. It is true – we already know this, but not only does the impact of this truth invite us to reflect, but also in this book we are shown short-cuts, sometimes fairy tale roads, little tricks that work from reiteration, so that we might conquer that autonomy, the one that we obtain by freeing ourselves of fear and its long trail. What happens inside each of us is decided by each of us, she says, mercilessly. I see myself sweetening this truth, because I will confess to you that I have been tempted to correct the words of the author in this way: "What happens inside each of us should be decided by oneself".

The conclusion is essential: allowing oneself to be carried away by future imperfects ('I *ought* to') will only give us stomach aches.

If we want to grow, we should take on responsibility and its risks. What prevents us from doing so? Fear. Fear of loneliness is another of the big ones, however deep and unacknowledged it might be. People are social animals; not only do we need one another in order to reproduce ourselves, eat, build, make our lives, in short, to survive, but we also need each other in order not to go mad.

Miriam Subirana goes much further; she goes to the shared essence, the place where we are all one, a vision that is shared by physics and biology. But she goes at street level, walking alongside the average person, so her reflection ends up as a practical piece of advice: We should control the impulse to be submissive and abandon our own personality in order to overcome the feeling of aloneness by submerging ourselves in the outer world. I am not only talking about the consumption of objects (and we might add people) but rather of external creativities such as television. In consuming only from without, our creativity and capacity to find creative solutions diminishes. And we become vulnerable.

The concepts in the book that have shaken me up personally are various. There is a specific phrase that was like a blow: your mind should obey you instantly. If we were serious, we would introduce this idea into schools. They are ferocious sentences: "Don't allow your mind to relive what is useless. Value your time. Value your creation: thoughts". But, best of all, in going through the pages, nothing of this seems unattainable, because it is pure logic, common sense and provocation.

With these brief examples one can already see that spirituality and action are inseparable for the author. The reality, she tells us, is that situations are not always as you would like them to be. It is in your hands to make your mental state more stable and stronger than situations, rather than the other way round, that situations determine your mental state. But Miriam Subirana does not abandon you there; she accompanies you along the path of practical meditation and reflection. It is worth reading this book again.

IMA SANCHÍS

INTRODUCTION

Living without fears and living with wholeness increases our quality of life and makes us happier. Where there is fear, there is no freedom and, without freedom, there is no happiness. Living without fears is a freedom experienced as an inner state that is free of negative influences, dependencies and habits that atrophy us emotionally and destroy our self-esteem and wholeness.

To live in wholeness is to be in a state in which the self shines; you are yourself and you dare to present yourself to the world with your singularities, your qualities and your differences. Your energy flows creatively, without blockages or fears.

During the day, a great part of our energy is spent on fears, on dependencies, on emotional reactions and on frustration. This waste of our energy is in all spheres of our lives, in our work and transactions, in our family life and relationships. You want to control the uncontrollable and you despair, you want to know where he is, who he is with. This need for control makes you anxious and fearful. You fear that things are not as you want, or will not go to plan. Fears fix your attention on certain things, excluding the rest. Your vision and your world are reduced. You lose global perspective. You drown in a glass of water.

In *The Way To Love* Anthony de Mello reminds us that: "You think wrongly that your fears protect you, that your beliefs have made you what you are and that your attachments make your life something exciting and strong. And you do not see that all of it constitutes a kind of screen or filter between you and the symphony of life".

This screen prevents you from enjoying yourself with wholeness and maintains your spiritual emptiness. All these tendencies take up a lot of your energy and do not give you happiness; rather they weaken you.

In your life there can be fears because you know there is a weakness, and at any moment it might emerge, leading you to failure, to feel rejected and alone.

However, when you plan to overcome your weaknesses and you do not achieve it, that makes you feel weaker, and you lose trust and self-esteem.

In this book I offer you methods with which to identify those weaknesses and fears that block you, and exercises or efforts that you can make to transform them by basing yourself on a greater understanding of yourself and your inner world. I go into the internal liberation necessary for you to develop all your potential and achieve wellbeing, happiness and wholeness. That is, to liberate yourself from the influences that deaden you, the kind that diminish your capacity to love, to shine, feel free and be at peace. They are external influences, but can also come from within you, such as the recordings of your past, your habits, your beliefs or your way of thinking. I offer a broad vision of the fears that cast shadows over your being and prevent you from flowing in life with love, serenity and trust.

In the first chapters I deal with the different fears that prevent you from enjoying life and how to overcome them. Then I go deeper into aspects that need to be taken into account in order to free yourself and be yourself: accepting and healing your past, changing certain habits, getting back your inner power and living out your values.

This will help you to live fully here and now, and learn to act motivated out of love, gratitude, peace, trust and co-operation.

That way you will generate an energy that attracts the positive and awakens enthusiasm and hope, because you are freeing yourself from the paralysis that fear brings on and beginning to be yourself, your creativity flows and you feel the strength to accept, confront and change.

Towards the end of the book you will find some meditations that will help you to create a space of silence in order to re-find yourself, become strong and be yourself.

That way you can enjoy wholeness in this present moment.

Don't waste an instant!

FEAR

"Everyone, when they are young, knows what their destiny is.
At that point in their lives, everything is clear and everything
is possible.
They are not afraid to dream, and to yearn for everything they
would like to see happen to them in their lives. But, as time
passes, a mysterious force begins to convince them that it will be
impossible for them to realize their destiny...
There is only one thing that makes a dream impossible to achieve:
the fear of failure".
Paulo Coelho, The Alchemist

Fear is a feeling that is generated by the lack of knowledge about a
certain situation, place or person. In fear, one feels threatened by
something real or imaginary.

Fear is an energy that puts a brake on you and prevents you
from doing what you want and aiming where you want to go. It
blocks you in the communication and expression of what you want
to say. Fear makes you hide, repress and not express the most
attractive, the most beautiful part of your being.

Fear has an influence on our capacity to reason, discern and
take decisions. It makes us doubt, it makes us indecisive even in
the most trivial decisions of our lives. Fear does not allow your
energy to flow, and that debilitates your state of wellbeing and
general health. Fear locks you into yourself and makes you become
indecisive. It is a shadow over your own being that prevents you
from acting with ease and fluidity. It reduces your capacity of
expression, of being yourself, of dealing with life and flowing in it.

Fear is an experience where there is anxiety, inhibition and
mistrust. Fear can lead us to aggressiveness and cynicism, to
depression, to illness, to defeat, to a lack of meaning in existence
and, eventually, to death.

Fear often shows itself in our lives in the form of stress, worries and anxiety. Stress is connected with feeling pressure, feeling pushed, forced, to meet deadlines, to do more. Having to produce more and more, and having to be better and better at it, generates tensions and worries that arise in the form of the fear of not being able to achieve those objectives or results on time. The materialistic values of achieving, obtaining, having, accumulating, and ambitions, competing and wanting to obtain a position, generate a lot of pressure and stress. When we are stressed, generally we are overcharged. We think, talk and react too much. All this affects the mind and body negatively. The worst thing is that it becomes a habit, often uncontrolled, so that the simple habit of stopping and relaxing is not considered a remedy. Some even consider it to be a waste of time. You have to do more and more, without stopping.

We have taken on stressful attitudes as part of our daily life. When stress persists, corticoids appear, these are sometimes called the 'fear hormones'. When released continuously, they affect our immune system, increasing the likelihood of cardiovascular complications and the risk of cancer.

When we do not have faith in our own capacity to resist pressure or difficulties, we feel insecure, and from insecurity the doors are opened for fears to enter. Sometimes, out of a lack of experience, self-knowledge or personal development, we are not aware of all the inner resources that we have. For example, if you do not trust your capacity to float in water, you drown. The body's density allows it to float automatically. Through not believing it, not knowing, or even knowing, when you panic, your strength to resist is reduced, your breathing becomes shallow and you may drown.

In February 2005 I was in India and I met a woman of about fifty-five who practiced meditation. She told me how she had never swum in her life, and yet, thanks to the trust she had developed in those years that she had been practicing meditation, she survived by floating for many hours in the waters shaken up by the Tsunami, in Sri Lanka, in December 2004. She had gone to the wedding celebration of a niece of hers, in a hotel on the coast of Sri Lanka, when they were hit by the Tsunami. Carried by the force of the water and floating between objects, tree trunks and other debris, she trusted in herself and in her capacity to survive, despite not knowing how to swim. Her faith gave her strength to survive.

We have many resources to be able to survive in times of crisis and many resources to live in wholeness in times of change. We simply have to discover them, recognize them and use them with trust.

The Fears We Have

We are all afraid of something. We all have fears at some point or other during our lives, and one fear brings about other fears. For example, the fear of death brings about the fear of illness or the fear of accidents. The fear of rejection comes from the fear of being perceived as different. The fear of success or standing out comes of the fear of relating to people. From the fear of failure comes the fear of making mistakes; the fear of taking on risks; the fear of taking decisions, the fear of not being recognized at work.

We are afraid of:
- Dying
- Getting ill
- The unknown
- Loneliness
- Other people
- Authority
- Being rejected
- Being hurt
- Failure
- Change
- The future
- Being
- Being free
- Thinking and being in a different way

- Losing control
- Dreaming and making our dreams real

From these fears many other fears and blockages emerge. The fear of others includes the fear of the anger and aggressiveness in others, fear that they might reject you, fear that they might judge you, and the violent feelings that this might cause you.

In this chapter I will deal with some of these fears and give some guidelines about how to understand, manage and overcome them.

Eliminating fears and liberating the mind requires a broad knowledge of how our mind and spirit work. Our spiritual conscience has to awaken for us to realize what the origin of our fears is and how to overcome them from the root.

Fears are like a tree; we can cut off a branch, but then others will grow, other fears. We have to go to the root and, even, the seed, to overcome the fears.

Understanding the Origin and Causes of Fear

We should understand the basis of fear, what it is that causes it and why we have it. Only if we understand it will we be able to overcome it. You can let go of your fears easily and rapidly when you know how to, without things having to change externally in order for you to eliminate your fears.

Ninety per cent of the causes of your fears are in your thinking. In order to recognize the fears, we should take note of the signals that they give us. Our feelings and our attitudes can reveal the fears that we hide. Certain feelings, such as happiness, gratitude, peace, trust or solidarity, inform us about what we have; naturally, they are pleasant feelings.

Other feelings inform us about something that we are lacking; they indicate an inner emptiness or deficiencies that exist inside us, such as sadness, fear, envy or blame. These emotions are, undoubtedly, painful and we usually say they are negative. But they are extremely valuable signs that direct us to problems that we are having in that moment. They are signs that, when under-stood, can allow us to bring about necessary change in our beliefs, attitudes and vision of situations, people, and, above all, ourselves.

For example, fear is the sensation of anguish that informs us that there is a lack of proportion between the threat that we think we face (often it is more a creation of our imagination than a reality, as we will see further on) and the resources that we have to deal with it. It is beneficial for us to identify the feelings that are behind the behavior and that are dangerous for our wellbeing and our health. The feelings that are the origin of our tensions and unhealthy habits comprise fears, anger and sadness. The feelings of fear encompass anguish, worries, stress, panic and phobias. Rage, hostility, fury and irritability are manifestations that one is beginning to enter a state of fear, anxiety and lack of control when the resources to adapt are insufficient, entering then into a dangerous state of vulnerability to illness, as Salvador García tells us. [1]

Fear invokes violence and it brings about blockages in our personal progress and in the construction of our self-esteem; it generates shyness, tension, a feeling of wanting to flee and nervous states, such as a raised heart rate, facial pallor, trembling voice.

Fear sets off a dance of hormones in our body, generating adrenalin, noradrenalin and corticoids, from which we end up by becoming ill. Being afraid creates short circuits in the neural connections. With fear we are less creative and we age more quickly.

Fear combined with feelings of guilt leads us to:
- Being incapable of maintaining positive thoughts.
- Being worried about the opinion of others.
- Having feelings of profound sadness.
- The loss of hope.
- Paranoia: when you think that others always have a negative vision of you.

Salvador García explains to us that the term "paranoia" could be translated as parallel thinking, or non-centered spirit. In this state people adopt a distant attitude in their social relationships that expresses itself basically in two ways: excessive politeness and charm, mixed with resistance, or an aggressiveness which may be shown directly or may be hidden under projections.

You should be careful with what you are afraid of, because you can invoke it.

Fear is like a magnet. **If you are afraid that something will happen to you and you get obsessed about it happening, you are effectively invoking it to happen.**

If you are very afraid that something might happen to you and you begin to visualize that it might happen or how it might happen, this terrifies you and it closes you into a phobia and a state of fear. What you are doing is invoking it to happen, because the power of the mind and visualization is very great. If you are afraid that you might be robbed, or of falling over, or of losing, you are invoking the robbery, the fall and the loss. Fear of rejection produces rejection.

That is how extraordinary the power of our mind is. That does not mean to say that we should not take the necessary precautions. A person of a certain age knows that to fall can mean their bones might break more easily. That person should not be preoccupied with a fear of falling; they simply need to apply attention and precaution when walking. But when precaution is confused with fear, it is not a healthy precaution or one that is free from worries.

One result of being afraid is **doubt**. When a person is lost in a sea of doubts, they cannot believe in the solutions and answers that come to mind, they are not even willing to try them and experiment with them to see if they work.

Doubts can go to the extreme of creating such uncertainty and insecurity that the person suffers paralysis or mental and emotional seizure. Then, they can enter a state of panic and become paralysed to the point of not finding the initiative to be positive. The mind is plagued with questions related to How? What? Why?

These questions are not asked in order to find answers but to prolong the doubts, or to remain on the defensive, or in a state of lack of commitment, where the person really does not want to listen or know.

Asking with the objective of being informed is different to these kinds of doubts.

When someone wants to be informed, they ask constructive questions with an openness to learn and willingness to experiment. When there is fear, expressed in the form of doubts, jealousy, secretiveness or a competitive attitude, there is no willingness to learn. At the heart of all this is the fear of loss, whether it be of a person, position, possession or one's own image. Fears cause dependence, expectations, and conflict with oneself or with others.

Fear can be caused by:

- Ignorance. When you don't know who your neighbour is, or when you don't know the intentions of the other, you are afraid. When you don't understand, you are afraid.
- A lack of inner preparation for the situation. For example, if you go unprepared to an exam, you will be afraid of failing it.
- A lack of clear knowledge on how to avoid or recognize situations that bring about actions that are dangerous for one's wellbeing.
- Insecurity in general and, specifically, about your qualities and your own capacity.
- Lack of faith in yourself.
- Mistrust.
- The inability to open oneself.
- The need to be recognized, appreciated and valued.
- Experiences of the past that have produced disappointment, insecurity, worry or emotional or mental exhaustion.
- The ego being afraid to 'die'. It justifies itself and resists. We wear masks that cover over our authentic identity. We become selfish.
- Attachments and dependencies generate fear.

- The habit of seeing situations and people in a negative way.
- Dishonesty. When you have done things that you know are not right, you know there will be repercussions, and this provokes fear within.

Sometimes, the original strong, authentic and shining self remains completely suffocated by a selfish self that represses and deadens, that provokes violence and aggression. Sometimes, on having bad thoughts, you feel fear or shame. Other times, however, it is about the best of your personality, whose repression is due to the fear of showing your feelings that are susceptible to being attacked or ridiculed by others.

We free ourselves from fear when we act with sincerity, without hypocrisy or deceit. Even if you have acted wrongly, if you have done things that you know are not right, if you have the power to realize it and to transform yourself, with the determination, the courage and the bravery to do what you know is right, then you will not be afraid. If you sow the seeds of the right action, then you won't have to be afraid of the future because right actions give their reward. Your conscience will be at peace and free of fear.

From the Outside In, or from the Inside Out?
Apart from these inner causes of fear, a general atmosphere of fear exists in the world. Due to human disasters or natural catastrophes, it seems that there is no place on earth where we can say that we are safe. There was a time when we used to say: "This place is not very safe, but you can be safe in that place". In recent years everything has changed so drastically that, on a physical level, there is practically no safe place.

It is said that there was a time when peace and non-violence reigned on earth, a utopia that is something like a myth. If a myth has survived hundreds of years and is universal, there must be some truth in it. For example, there is a universal story that appears in the writings of the East and West, of a time when lions and lambs drank together at the same water. Something changed in humanity and it stopped being the era of non-violence, and violence began. But even so they followed some rules and disciplines in war. In the *Mahabharat* [2] which is one of the oldest sacred books of India, it is explained that there was great chaos and much evil in the world. The Pandavas and the Kauravas fought each other during the day but at night they had dinner together. So there was a time when, even in war, there was a rule about how one was involved in the war and how one went about it.

A friend who went to New Zealand explained to me that she discovered that in the past, although there was war, certain disciplines were followed. They followed a principle: that the enemy would attack from the front, not from behind.The indigenous people born there, the Maoris, explained that only the part in front of the village was fortified; there weren't any fortifications behind.

But nowadays there is violence everywhere, not only in the battlefield. The whole world has become a battlefield. So that, as we see violence grow, fear grows. Today, you travel by bus or on the underground, in London, Bagdad or Madrid, or in another big city, and a bomb might go off. You can go into a supermarket and a bomb might go off.

One of the fastest growing businesses is security. You can put more locks on your doors, install more alarm systems. You can have all the external security in the world, but fear does not necessarily go away because of it. We carry fear within and it has nothing to do with how many locks you put on the door of your house. Instead of peace, we are surrounded by a lot of violence, and we carry it inside us as well. What is happening? What has happened to the world? How is it that the world has gone mad?

There is a spiritual law that says that what **happens within is reflected on the outside** and when there is inner conflict it expresses itself externally. Peace treaties are signed, lectures and congresses for peace are organized and even so there is not peace within us. **It is not the external answers that will give us a solution. It is the inner answers which will help us to solve the situations on the outside.**

When there is conflict on the outside, one of the solutions we try to apply is dialogue. When the conflict is inside us, the solution is also in dialogue. The dialogue between heart and mind. The dialogue of reason and conscience. The dialogue between your feelings and reasoning based on logic and spiritual intelligence. It means turning inwards to see yourself within and trying to resolve all the inner conflicts. This is possible. It is possible to go within and solve the conflict, and reach a state of stability and peace. When you connect with your true self, with the authenticity of what you are in reality, in that consciousness you are not afraid. There is peace, calm and serenity.

Our psychological destiny will depend on the relationship that we establish between heart and mind; it might be a road where dissatisfaction and suffering reign or, on the contrary, a road that we walk peacefully, learning and with the emotional peace that is produced by acting with the wisdom of spiritual and emotional intelligence.

If you are brave, if you are not afraid inside, the power of the vibration that you emanate can change things on the outside. This can happen in any situation and in any place or city in the world. For example, it happened in Sao Paolo. Some years ago, there was an event with hundreds of people who had gone to listen to spiritual teachings on a theme to do with peace and non-violence in personal development.

The next morning we had a group meditation. One of the women shared her experience from the day before. She explained how after the event she had gone to get her car, she got in and wound the window down. When she tried to put it up again, she realized that it was stuck and that she couldn't get it up. On turning round, she saw that a gun was being pointed at her. A young man of eighteen or nineteen was pointing the weapon at her and demanding her bag, her money. She didn't have her bag or her money with her, because she had gone to a spiritual conference and hadn't taken anything with her. She was with a friend who didn't have anything either. In that moment the question in her mind was, "What should I do?" and for a moment she was afraid.

In an instant she remembered what she had just heard at the conference about the power of peace. At that moment of touch and go, the power of peace manifested itself. After the presentation they had shared out some biscuits that were very nicely wrapped. In a second she thought: "I haven't got my bag, I haven't got any money, what should I do? I have this biscuit!" She picked up the biscuit and with a big smile she said to him:

"I haven't got any money, I haven't brought my bag, but I have this to give you."

As she gave this young man the biscuit, she looked him straight in the eyes and shared with him the power of peace. That peace touched the young man and he began to smile. He took the biscuit and he left.

The next morning, she told us about this experience. Imagine what would have happened if she had been afraid and her nervousness had pervaded this situation. The vibration of fear would have touched the man and who knows what could have happened. The power of vibrations works.

Just as the power of fear is contagious, the power of peace also reaches others.

On another occasion, a friend who is a teacher of meditation and developing a positive attitude in life, explained to me what happened to her when she was a participant in a program being filmed for television. The subject of the program was "What have you experienced in relation to the power of positivism?" The moderator was a well-known television figure. There were around 500 people in the audience. Also participating on the round table were a sportsman and Dr Brian Weiss, who had written a book on past lives called *Many Lives, Many Masters*.

At the end of the program, the moderator asked if anyone wanted to ask a question.

A middle-aged woman, well dressed, said that she wanted to share an experience. The woman explained that she had been at a party on the beach and the time had come to go home. She was driving alone towards her home, late at night. She was going through a dodgy neighbourhood when her car stopped. She hadn't realized that she was running on reserve and she had no petrol left. It was two o'clock in the morning, she was alone, and had no petrol in the car, and was wondering what to do. She was sitting there when she saw two big men coming towards the car.

At that moment this question came into her mind: "Now what?"

The thought came to her: "**You can choose the situation that you want**".

She got out of the car and went running towards these two men; she embraced them and said to them, "Thank you, God must have sent you to help me." And if someone embraces you and invokes God's name, what are you going to do? You are going to smile. So, they said to her: "What can we do, what is the problem?" She explained and one of them got an empty can to go and fill it with petrol some two or three kilometres away and the other one sat in the car with her to protect her. The man brought the petrol, he gave it to her and then they left. She went home.

These are examples of how the **power of love conquers fear and conquers violence**.

I am talking about real situations that people have lived through and shared. When there is an awareness that we are the creators and when we are aware of the protection of God, fear goes.

Identify your Hidden Fears

If you want to overcome fears, you have to commit yourself to investigating your feelings and emotions in order to know them, and thus know how to manage them and correct them or overcome them.

If you know what to do to achieve your objectives, but even then do not do so, it is possible that you are afraid of something. There is a simple exercise that you can do to help you identify those subtle and sometimes unconscious fears. Choose an area of your life that you feel stuck in. Ask yourself these three questions:

    1.   What do I really want?

2. What obstacle/s is/are getting in my way?
3. What prevents me from dealing with or overcoming that obstacle?

For each fear that comes to you in response to the third question, ask yourself the following questions:

1. What is the worst that can happen if what I am afraid of occurs?
2. What is the best possible outcome for me or for others, if I do it even though I feel afraid of doing it?
3. What might possibly happen of these two things?

I recommend that you try any potentially worthy activity, at least three times: one to learn to do it; the second to overcome the fear of doing it; and the third time to find out if you really enjoy it or not!

There are things that you are perhaps afraid of doing, but that you know it is good to do. For example, if you are afraid of speaking in public or to a group. How do you overcome this fear? By speaking in a group. You speak and you realize that it is not a problem. Even if you make a mistake or stammer a little or you feel unsure, with practice you will see that there is no problem.

There are some fears that are overcome with the practice of doing what you are afraid of, as long as it is something positive and worthwhile. If you do not make a brave move in order to overcome the fear of expressing yourself, you will continue to be the victim of this fear that disorganizes your ideas and makes you lose the thread when you express yourself. What is more, fear produces verbal clumsiness and makes a speaker lose their image of credibility. You have to overcome it, and you will manage to do it with practice and by changing the vision that you have of others: they are not a threat, they are not judges, they are offering you the opportunity to express yourself; if you value yourself, you will not be afraid of not being appreciated by them.

When you are **afraid of failure**, for example when going to a work interview or faced with someone, it may be due to a personal insecurity. You have to work on it in order to have more security and firmness. Being secure in the moment of communicating and expressing yourself requires training, practice and effort. You have to value yourself. If you value yourself, it does not matter so much to you whether another values you or not. However, if you aren't able to value yourself, the doubt exists: "Let's see if this person values me"; "perhaps this is not for me"; "perhaps I am no good at this". Then you need recognition and appreciation. You depend on others giving it to you.

You need to know that you are unique and that you are worth a great deal.

If the other person does not value you it is their problem, their loss; they are losing a treasure. If you go with that self esteem and that awareness – Here comes a treasure to interview you, your words and your attitude will be firm, secure and stable. Within you, you value yourself; and if you value yourself, it will be easier for people to value you. On the other hand, if you despise yourself, you will invoke the despising of others.

It is strange, isn't it? There are people very much in need of love but they invoke the opposite, because as they do not love themselves and sometimes even hate themselves, they invoke that negativity and do not appreciate or open themselves to receive the love that is offered to them.

Failure is directly related to our expectations of success. And the concept of success varies greatly from one person to another. Choosing what is success for us is an exercise in freedom. We ourselves set the goals that we wish to reach or the objectives that supposedly would make us feel ourselves to be without fear. The fear of failure appears when we make an effort to achieve those goals and we sabotage the result without wanting to because of our fears.

Whenever you feel that you have failed, have a positive and learning attitude. That way your creative energy will flow and you will carry on going forward without the failure (apparent or real) blocking you or preventing you from doing so. Although it may seem as though you have missed an opportunity or that some doors have closed for you, have faith, trust, because other possibilities will open up.

We believe and are conditioned to think that our fear will keep us safe, and we treat it like a red light, a signal that tells us that we should stop.

Creating a time every day to do something that you fear or that you feel a little insecure or nervous about, helps you to recondition yourself internally to begin to see the fear as a green light and to develop inner courage and bravery.

"Every day do something that you are afraid of
Do what you fear and the death of the fear is assured."
Eleanor Roosevelt

IGNORANCE AND INNER EMPTINESS

"Ignorance is the mother of fear"
Henry Home Kames, philosopher (1696-1782)

Ignorance and lack of knowledge drive you to fear. When you do not know who your neighbor is, you are afraid. I am referring to a neighbor in your community, in your neighborhood, in your country, in the world. When you don't know the one who is different, of another religion, of other customs and beliefs, or of another skin colour, and you do not know what their intentions are, you are afraid. Because when you don't know, the human mind is very fertile, very creative, and all kinds of things can arise within it. But if you take care to find out and to understand, fear can be overcome.

There are old people who are afraid of computers and yet, a child of four already plays with computers. The difference is that the person who doesn't know about them is afraid, and the child who is curious wants to discover and play, getting to know how they work. Ignorance, with the problems and fears that it provokes, is a matter that can be applied to all areas of life.

It is important to take on the commitment to recognize, manage and overcome our fears, because if not we will be the victims of our mental and emotional ignorance.

Ignorance is the basic cause of all badness. When there is ignorance and you don't know your spiritual identity, there is ego, fear, attachment, greed, anger, lechery and laziness. When you do not know your being, your spiritual identity, neither do you see the other as a spiritual being and you only see external aspects, which generates divisions, racism and misunderstanding. Fear can enter relationships. When you know yourself and you know others, a relationship is awoken that is eternal, where love flows without fears.

Your World Is As Your Vision Is

As Anthony de Mello says: "You see people and things not as they are, but as you are. If you want to see them as they are, you should pay attention to your attachments and to the fears that they engender. Because, when you are face to face with life, it is those attachments and those fears that decide what it is that you have to see and what you have to ignore. And whatever it is that you see, it will take up your attention. Now, as your look is selective, you have a deceptive vision of the things and people that surround you. And the longer this deformed vision lasts, the more you will convince yourself that that is the true image of the world, because your attachments and your fears continue to process new data that reinforces the given image. This is what makes up the origin of your beliefs, which are only fixed and immutable ways of looking at a reality that, in itself, is not fixed or immutable, but rather mobile and in constant change. Thus, the world that you relate to and that you love is no longer the real world, but a world created by your own mind. Only when you manage to renounce your beliefs, your fears and the attachments that give rise to them, will you see yourself as free of that lack of sensitivity that makes you so deaf and blind towards yourself and towards the world." [3]

To heal that "deafness and blindness" and understand the origin and cause of fears, we need to know the identity of the self, that is, how our internal mechanisms work and what we identify with. That is, to know how to answer the question "Who am I?"

To go even deeper, we should also understand the law of karma, understand God, and how we create our destiny as we go along. Those who are aware of these concepts and awaken to the truth that they shelter can free themselves of fears. Because fear arises basically out of ignorance. We ignore our true self. We ignore God, and thus we are also ignorant about the lives of others and the common destiny that we share.

Deficiencies and Greed

Deficiencies bring about the greed that arises out of the spiritual void, of the lack of wholeness. As we act by basing ourselves on these human weaknesses, the result is suffering, sorrow and pain. If we were to act according to the human and spiritual values, virtues and qualities, the result would be cooperation, solidarity, happiness, joy, peace, wellbeing and, finally, wholeness.

When there is selfishness, there is greed. We want to have more and possess more, which generates a state of expectation and anxiety. We fill our lives with things and objects to cover up deeper deficiencies. Then we are afraid of losing them. We generate expectations of all kinds, and when they are not fulfilled we react with anger, frustration or disappointment. The inner emptiness makes us become greedy, and this brings about imbalances in oneself, in relation to others, and between human beings and nature. We fill ourselves with objects, properties, things. We take and consume more than nature can give, and we pollute more than nature is able to recycle.

Something similar happens to the body, which is a mini-cosmos. The body has a capacity to recycle and eliminate waste through the pores of the skin, the nose, defecating, urinating, etc. we get rid of all the waste, everything that the body does not need. However, since we consume more toxins than the body can process, we are more prone to feeling bad, to developing tumours and getting ill.

Greed, selfishness, attachment and dependencies are the roots that bring about a great imbalance on a world scale, and also on a local scale. Greed acts on various levels: personal, interpersonal, on the level of the behaviour of companies and on a national and international level. Out of greed many companies and their bosses are not prepared to modify their activity in order to reduce the emission of gases and waste products that pollute the environment and are destroying the environmental balance. They are endangering the planet, our existence and the life of many animals and live beings. However, because of their greed, they do not change. Our greed leads us to consume in an imbalanced way. Companies prefer to pay a fine rather than reduce toxic gases or the pollution that they throw into the rivers and the atmosphere in order to be able to continue producing at the same volume with minimal economic costs, although it is at greater cost at another level (pollution, global warming and environmental imbalance).

In sum, what does all this show us? That greed leads us to a lack of respect towards ourselves, others, animals and the environment. Greed generates desires for power and the fear of change.

Out of selfishness and greed there is a fight for power. When an individual feels spiritually whole, he/she has a stable inner power that he/she does not need to defend and has no fear of losing it. To the extent that an individual is powerful, that is, able to realize their potential basing themselves on freedom and the integrity of the true self, of being, they do not need to dominate and find themselves without the appetite for power.

Control and Power

We believe that we can control people and situations. However, there are many things that we cannot control. Neither can we control people, and when we want to control them a clash takes place. In many cases, when dependence has been generated within relationships, there is control and submission. This generates an enormous unhappiness, and even then people hold on to their dependencies.

Because of this, Erich Fromm posed the question: "Might there not exist perhaps, together with an innate desire for freedom, an instinctive desire for submission? And if this doesn't exist, how can we explain the attraction that submission to a leader holds for so many people?" The submission to a hero, the submission to a guru, a leader, or any person who "represents" something? Will submission always happen in relation to an external authority, or does there also exist a relationship with authorities that has been internalised, such as duty or conscience, or in relation to the coercion exercised by intimate impulses, or in the face of anonymous authorities such as public opinion? Does there perhaps exist a hidden satisfaction in submission? And if there does, what does it consist of? What is it that provokes in man an insatiable appetite for power?" [4]

The fear of authority can be of a father or mother, a boss, a teacher, or even of God. Frequently, authority has been misused or represented badly, in order to control or oppress people, and as a consequence, fear, in the form of suspicion and mistrust, has turned into a negative force in society, both on a personal and collective level.

Out of insecurity, as human beings we exercise the power of wanting to control others by causing fear in them. We want to control our children, control the traffic, control time, control that there are no jellyfish in the sea when we want to go swimming.[5]

We want to control space, the moon, and yet we are incapable of controlling what is happening inside us. We are not capable of controlling our own minds.

Many corporations still work with the old scheme of exercising power and controlling by generating fear, submission and repression. The bosses are stuck to their armchair of power. Power is a drug. It is difficult to get unused to it. "Influencing the lives of others relieves us of our own doubts," as Erich Fromm said. When people are obliged to pay you attention, you have the option of rewarding or penalizing. Power over others has a positive effect on one's own insecurities.

The fear of the loss of power appears in those who are driven to influence others or to have submissive people who can be controlled and dominated. Possibly, even more so than in politics, it is most important in the world of management, although it is not openly recognized. From the fear of the loss of power derives the fear of losing a position of influence and the fear of not being socially recognized.

The ego, understood as a limited identity of the bodily self, makes us think and feel that objects, people, lands and many other things are "ours". Those feelings are extended on a national and international level: "This part of the sea is ours" and "this part of the sky is ours". When the air traffic controllers go on strike, or when there are wars or other situations of disagreement and conflict, it is not possible to fly in one part of the sky or air space, and you have to fly in another part as if the sky were private property.

It is true that for the functioning and organization of our lives, commerce and exchange, we need certain laws and definition of spaces. But we should not forget that attaching ourselves to this leads us to violent reactions. Beyond this reality there exists another more important one: spiritual reality.

The ego has led us to believe that a person can belong to us as if they were private property, due to the fact that we gave birth to them or are married to them. When the feeling of possession exists, when we believe that this person, this chair, this job, this car, is ours, automatically we are afraid of losing them or that someone might take them from us. That awareness of *mine* leads us to the fear of losing what is ours and, automatically, that makes us defend the rights to what we believe is ours. When this defence is made out of fear and possession, violent reactions can occur. I am not saying that everything belongs to everyone and there should be a lack of control. It is a question of inner awareness: that selfish feeling that leads us to want to have more and to feel that what we are worth depends on how much we have, not what we are and the quality of what we are. That attitude, that thought and that feeling, based on the belief that "I am worth what I have", leave us with a profound inner emptiness and bring about fears, attachments, anger and violence. The obsession for control is usually based on mistrust, the lack of genuine self-esteem, insecurity and the fear of uncertainty and freedom. Taken to an extreme, it means an aversion to risk, resistance to change and the inhibition of our own creativity and that of others. The obsession for control arises out of the inability to recognize and appreciate the value of spontaneity and joy.

"The lesser the trust, the more need for control. The conventional hierarchical company is based on an excess of desire for control based on fear and insecurity. Without trust, fear causes the structures of control to hypertrophy and generates systems that are not very fluid, bureaucratic, slow, sad, repetitive, predictable and, in sum, inefficient and emotionally atrophying." [6]

Being Safe

There is another aspect connected to the feeling of security and fear. When we were children, we were taught to fear things in order to keep us safe. Instead of explaining the dangers that we might find in this world, our parents or guardians taught us to generate fear as a "survival" technique, as a way of protecting us and keeping us safe. Thus we have inherited the almost global belief that fear is what keeps us safe.

In fact, **what keeps us safe is intelligence**. What would be useful would be for someone to explain it all to us, not as if the child were stupid or careless or automatically heading for disaster, but rather as a way of giving information to someone who doesn't have it.

Fear is not a true or real indicator that there is a danger nor that one is approaching. Never think that because you are afraid of something, that fear is a warning and will keep you safe. In fact, it is good decisions that will keep you safe and that will give you inner security and confidence in yourself.

Fear, Rejection and Violence

In our present-day society we are suffering from an increase in violence. Violence is expressed in many ways. One of them is violence towards oneself and it can bring on illnesses that are created internally by the self when it is dominated by fears and by anger. When we feel fear, we segregate hormones, as if we were preparing ourselves for flight or to attack. Those hormones often continue circulating around the body causing illnesses such as: hypertension, stomach ulcers, heart disease, etc.

Violence can also appear as a form of mental incapacity to activate creative responses in the brain, and in the mind. This takes the form of depression, or manic depression in some cases. Then, there is a violent behavior whereby we project our feelings of deficiency, of insecurity onto others.

These is also an increase of arbitrary violence, not only the organized kind. What I mean by arbitrary violence is that it seems to be sudden and not premeditated. Shootings, gangs of youths who alone would not attack anybody, given that the people of that group normally are quite passive. As soon as they are in the group, something comes up in their mass consciousness within the group, and their behavior becomes violent. Perhaps at the heart of this is insecurity, the fear of rejection or of being left alone. There is a need to link up with others. Perhaps some of the leaders of the group project their pains and sorrows onto other people. They become a focus where they can violently release all that anguish.

We are afraid of not belonging, we are afraid of being rejected. This fear arises from the necessity to belong to a group. It is stronger in young people when peer pressure and the approval of the rest is sought and it is not well looked on to stand out or be different.

This fear turns us into people under submission, dependent and addicted. And those young people, linking up to certain groups, become violent. And who are those most enslaved to the fear of rejection? Those who most need to belong to a group, those with an affiliate motivation who take refuge in the group from the loneliness they are fleeing.

Socially, rejection generates violence. The fear of rejection works in such a way that you amplify the experience of rejection and you generate anger against yourself or against others. The corresponding attitude to attack is that of aggression. Social fear is increasing, and from there so do aggressive attitudes. Aggressiveness takes on many modes. For example, rudeness or harassment.

The fear of rejection is painful and addictive at the same time. Rejection hurts and it generates anger and desires for revenge. The one who is rejected will find it difficult to move away emotionally from the life of the person who they were rejected by.

The ultimate origin of this violent behaviour is that the soul was not nourished in the way that it needed to be: loved, cared for, respected, valued. Now a great effort has to be made to be capable of maintaining a balanced and healthy mind and to strengthen its bases in order to build a solid and lasting self-esteem.

ALONENESS AND FREEDOM

Anthony de Mello[7] states that in aloneness lies freedom. In aloneness is life. In not clinging is the decision to flow freely, to enjoy, like and savour each new instant of life; a life that is now much sweeter, because it has remained free of unrest, tension and insecurity; free of the fear of loss and death that always accompanies the desire to stay and cling on.

We have a freedom that provides us with independence, rationality and a critical capacity. However, we feel alone and isolated in the face of this globalized world that, although it offers us many measures that facilitate the freedom of choice and communication, terrifies us and makes us feel impotent in the face of all the challenges that it implies. We feel fascinated by the growing freedom that we acquire at the expense of resources, commodities and external powers, and we blind ourselves to the fact of restriction, anguish and inner fears.

Feeling alone generates an anguish that is sometimes unbearable. We have the alternative of fleeing from the responsibility that freedom offers us, generating different forms of dependence and submission, or rather, progressing to the complete realisation of freedom, reaching wholeness and personal development, and enjoying solitude out of wholeness. As human beings we need to relate to the outside world and thus avoid isolation and loneliness. It is not possible for a human being to be alone on an island. Even in the days when there were many monks and nuns separating themselves from society, society supported them, meaning that they were not totally isolated.

Sometimes we isolate ourselves out of fear of others, of being hurt, of being different, of being rejected, amongst other fears. When we isolate ourselves, we run the risk of experiencing an internal imbalance or a mental disintegration. The problem is not so much physical aloneness but rather moral aloneness. One can be alone in the physical sense but have a spiritually rich inner world and be related to ideas, values or, at least, social norms that provide one with a feeling of community and "belonging". On the other hand, one can live amongst people and allow oneself to be overcome by a feeling of total isolation due to the lack of connection with values, symbols or norms, due to the incapacity for communication and a feeling of weakness, anguish and impotence.

It is not so much being with people that helps us to overcome the feeling of aloneness but rather that the greater the connection based on values and spiritual content, the greater the feeling of belonging to the human family and global community.

Religious people, artists and writers, amongst others, often love solitude, but they do not feel alone: they are united to other people through beliefs, symbols or values. The political prisoner isolated from others feels united with their companions in the struggle and does not feel morally alone.

To come out of this state of loneliness and impotence we should progress towards the positive freedom that independence and a critical and reflexive capacity offer us; they give us confidence in ourselves. This allows us the realisation of our individual self, the expression of our intellectual, emotional and sensitive potential, that is, the development of the spiritual self and the growth of an active, critical, creative and responsible self. We should control the impulse to be submissive and abandon our own personality in order to overcome the feeling of loneliness and impotence by submerging ourselves in the outside world. This makes us become extrovert and we do not take care of our personal development. We lose contact with that which is essential. We make the outside world responsible for how we feel inside, since, on being submissive, we have given it the power to take our life decisions.

We hide our loneliness with the daily routine of activities, security and approval that we find in private and social relation-ships, success at work or in business, or in any form that ultimately implies a distraction. But whistling in the dark does not bring light. The loneliness, the fear and the anguish remain. Then, the person insecure of themselves cannot carry the weight that freedom imposes on them; they have to try to escape from it by looking for avoidance mechanisms if they don't manage to progress from negative freedom to the positive (responsible for their own decisions and acts). The main collective forms of evasion in our time are represented by the submission to a leader, a guru, to football, to the pleasures of the senses, to excessive consumption. The individual forms of evasion would be those that one depends on and is addicted to - gambling, sex, drugs or alcohol, amongst other objects of addiction.

The state of loneliness, insecurity and impotence when an inner emptiness is produced and creativity and the emotions are "atrophied", at times becomes unbearable. To overcome it, one has two options: to overcome this situation or succumb to it. With the first you are able to progress towards "positive freedom", whereby you take on your personal government and can establish your connection with the world of love and work spontaneously, in the genuine expression of your emotional, feeling and intellectual facilities: in this way, you will join humanity, nature and yourself again, without stripping yourself of the integrity and independence of your individual and unique self. With the other option you go backwards; you give up your freedom and you try to overcome the loneliness by eliminating the gap that has opened up between your individual personality and the world, generating dependencies, addictions and a considerable mental and emotional imbalance.

If a person is not mentally stable, they are not emotionally strong, they do not have balance and they have not nourished themselves spiritually, although they have all this range of possible freedoms; they feel alone, insecure and with inner deficiencies. Often they try to fill this emptiness through consumption. Not only the consumption of products, objects and properties, but also the consumption of the creativity of the other. When you go to see a film, you consume the creativity of other people, you are a consumer, not a creator; the same occurs when you are watching television. I am not saying it is bad to watch films. Simply, one should be aware of not avoiding and running from oneself. We become the consumers of others' creativity and with this our mind also atrophies, since we don't use our creativity to enrich moments of solitude. As aloneness bores or even panics us, we switch on the television or the radio. There are people who have the radio on all day, to hear a voice to keep them company, although in reality they are not listening to it.

In fact, we increase that spiritual, existential emptiness, because we have confused our identity and we have identified with things that are external to us. In only consuming from the outside, our creativity and capacity to find creative solutions has diminished. All this has generated a vulnerability that has opened us to consume pain and disappointment, to suffer and become sad.

* * *

In the present day, especially in western societies, we have many resources and facilities, and there has been liberation in relation to human relationships: whether you are married, or divorced, whether you get married again, if you do not, if you are with two people, with three, or alone. A great range of choices and possibilities exist that, not so long ago, were difficult to imagine. Societies were much more restricted and lived under the imposition of the Church or, in other countries, other regimes or institutions. The weight of tradition was very strong and acted as an impediment to living out the concept of freedom in its widest sense.

In spite of the great freedom that as individuals, as human beings and as a collective, we have gained, the experience of fear and pain seems to have increased, because we have not known how to use this freedom to strengthen ourselves emotionally, mentally and spiritually. Out of the fear of feeling more pain, we close off our hearts and remain blocked.

No human being can satisfy our deepest deficiencies. They might be able to help us in some circumstances but, at bottom, the reality is that we are alone.

If I do not want anything from anybody, I will not be afraid. If others want to share with me, fine, and if not, also fine. That greed of wanting attention, wanting respect, wanting love, leaves us in a state of permanent emptiness.

I am not afraid of aloneness, because my aloneness is very creative, where there is a communication with God and with humanity. An aloneness where I can know myself, meditate, study, paint, draw, write, that is, in which I can create on many positive levels.

When you create that state of love for yourself and for others, you are not afraid of being with many people or of being alone. The person able to be alone is able to be with many people, because, in being fine with themselves, they are fine with anyone else.

On the other hand, if you can only be with three people or with three kinds of personalities, because you don't get on with the others or you get angry or they irritate you, you are in a state of dependency that leads you to the fear of losing those people that you are fine with or fear that the situation might change, and you generate a controlling energy to prevent changes.

LOVE OR DEPENDENCE

Relationships are a source of support for our life, or at least, they should be. Relationships suppose an exchange of happiness and love. Harmonious relationships are the basis from where to create, generate and carry out shared projects. Thanks to cooperation, we achieve our objectives.

When I ask people what the different factors are that cause stress, worries and suffering, one of the main answers is relationships. Relationships have become a cause of ties and pain. Instead of trust it seems fear dominates. In a relationship of love – be it family, be it friendship – fear prevents us from developing and expressing all our potential, meaning that we stop being ourselves and we fear sharing ourselves openly. Due to emotional deficiencies and a lack of self-esteem, in order to learn to love ourselves we need another person or people to value us, to appreciate us, to need us, to love us. Even so, we do not manage to learn to love ourselves and we continue to depend on and worry about the opinion of others, what others might say, think or feel about us. You fear the answer of others; you fear they might say something that hurts you. These fears arise out of the emotional and affective dependence on this person or these people.

With this dependency we enter into a dynamic of pleasing others so that they might continue to appreciate us. We base our self-esteem and personal security on the appreciation of these people. We stop acting in a natural, free and spontaneous way because we are worried about pleasing the one from whom we are taking support, be it mental, emotional or physical.

Into this dynamic of dependence enters fear: fear of losing the support of that person, fear they will get angry, fear they will stop supporting us, fear that they might not like us any more, fear that they might reject us, etc. That fear is a signal that warns us of our emotional deficiencies and of our lack of self-esteem. Fear brings on a greater inner insecurity, which makes us carry on leaning on that dependence.

There are people who, after entering into a dynamic of dependence and suffering because of it, leave that relationship with the objective of freeing themselves from the anguish it brings about in them. Then they begin another relationship, where they generate the same dynamic. The solution is not in a change of relationship with another person, although on occasion that might help us. If we don't change this dynamic internally and if we don't learn to have a solid base of self-esteem, we will continue to depend on the appreciation and affection of others in order to appreciate and love ourselves.

Unless we learn and manage to free ourselves of this tendency towards dependence, we will continue to have affective and emotional deficiencies, and an inner emptiness. Although we feel that that person we depend on fills us, ultimately it is a mirage. In reality, something remains of the emptiness, unsatisfied expectation or fear of rejection or loss within us. We have to be attentive in order to realize the vicious circle that this represents. When a deficiency exists in our being – whether it is an emotional deficiency or a lack of self-esteem – we try to fill it with a dependency. We try to satisfy our deficiencies by depending on someone who fills us or who it seems to us might fill us. By depending on someone it is as if we gave that person permission to manage, dominate and enter into our heart and our life to the point that, in some moments, we feel vulnerable, wounded or disappointed by them.

We should learn to love ourselves in order not to continue depending on others and worrying about their opinion. No person can satisfy our deficiencies one hundred per cent. One person will help us in one aspect, someone else in another, but when the relationship turns into a dependency and a tie, that help turns against us. As a result, fear appears, which expresses itself in the form of worries, anxiety, anguish and tension. These emotions always arise out of some form of attachment and not only do they exhaust our energy, but, in time, they pollute our relationships.

Wherever we find the negative energy of such emotions in our life, the solution is always to detach ourselves.

It depends on you what you consume, what you make of your life and how you focus it. What happens inside each one of us we decide for ourselves, as long as we do not have dependencies to the point of allowing other people to influence us. Dependencies make us allow these people to be in charge in our lives. You have collaborated in them being generated, and you are allowing it, and you continue feeding off the dependency. So don't complain about your own creation. Reflect upon what happens with your love. If you are with a person who (out of love) stifles you, controls you and makes demands on you, how much are you going to put up with it and at what price? You can be free and happy. If there is not freedom there is not happiness. What sense does it make to live embittered all your life?

We need to learn the art of loving and being free, without fear, without frustrations.

To do so you need to cultivate the art of flexibility, of adapting yourself to change. You have to be tolerant, which does not mean putting up with, but rather understanding, the other and adapting yourself to the situation without losing your own integrity and dignity. If to adapt yourself to the situation or another person, to their demands, their dependencies, you have to lose your dignity, that is falling under their influence; it can even become submission, where you are in the state of victim. Is it possible to love each other and be free at the same time? Yes. To reach this state in a relationship a great wisdom is required. Most people love one another and tie one another down. Thus they lose their freedom. When freedom is lost, happiness retreats, and true wellbeing gives way to unhappiness. Often we look above all for love, a love we believe will change our life. We see it as the virtuous recognition of our intrinsic value by another person. However, we trip over ourselves in looking for this love. Necessity is what moves us. We project our need by making an incursion into the world, and we try to satisfy it with an object or person who matches up to perfection.

We have an enormous emotional need for love, and the fear of remaining in a state of unsatisfied wanting. In our search to fill our need, we are prepared to deceive ourselves with unsuitable partners. Many people allow the love of another person to define their personality to such a point that, if they are rejected, they lose any sense of who they are and of the purpose they have in life. Often the relationship is marked, through one of the partners or both, by fear.

To free ourselves of the tendency to depend, we should have a strong heart, capable of repudiating its selfishness; a heart that has nothing to hide and that, as a consequence, leaves the mind free and without fear; a heart that is always prepared to accept new information and change its mind, that does not cling on to closed beliefs, to obsolete data. A heart that cultivates good feelings, free of bitterness. Cultivating the true values of peace, serenity, love, freedom and solidarity, we will overcome the deficiencies, we will feel stronger and we will reach wholeness. A heart like that ends up turning into a lamp that dissipates the dark.

This understanding of the polarity of love and fear has been at the heart of the world's ancient wisdoms for thousands of years. However, it has been clouded by the modern religion of consumerism and the idea that in order to be happy we must acquire "things" and form relationships of attachment to them. Entertainment industries sustain the illusion that in order to find love we must possess or be attached to the other person. This confusion between love and attachment has been translated into all our relationships in a number of ways.

To our conditioned minds it appears to be a paradox, but it is a basic spiritual truth – to be loving it is necessary to be detached. Attachment is the root of fear and fear and love cannot co-exist just as day and night, winter and summer cannot, says Mike George in *In the Light of Meditation*. The idea and the practice of detachment are found at the heart of almost all the paths of wisdom, over the centuries. This is so because attachment is one of the deepest habits that we learn to develop, and we do not realize that anything we attach ourselves to turns into a trap for our consciousness, for the self, the being. We know we are attached when we begin to think about someone or something when they are not present and there is no need to think about them. Our mental energy exhausts itself and we have the sensation that we lack control over our thoughts and feelings.

Each time that we automatically cling to something, we invoke the presence of fear. Whether it be of people, position, power, money or even opinion, any form of attachment means that we will fear harm or loss. Fear takes on many faces (worry, anxiety, and tension); it prevents our spiritual growth and frightens us away from or blocks us from love.

Detachment is the basis of our capacity to be positive and affectionate with others while we interact with them. This is what is known as commitment and the relationship of detachment and it begins with what is known as a spiritual skill: the skill of being a detached observer. Being a detached observer implies the existence of two dimensions: one within and one without. The inner art of detached observation is the faculty of separating ourselves from our own thoughts, emotions, attitudes and behavior.

On the most superficial level, the art of detached observation is the art of being witness to the scenes that take place around us. While we detach ourselves and observe how the game of life develops, without being active participants, we are able to see the "big picture" with greater clarity. That makes it easier to discern clearly what role we have to play and where our contribution lies.

We are creators, and our thoughts, emotions and attitudes are our own work.

In reality, it is the first step towards personal strengthening. Whilst we don't manage to detach ourselves from our thoughts and emotions, they will turn into our owners and will consume our energy.

For the practice of meditation it is essential that you act as a witness of everything you think and feel, and, once some time has passed, you will find that the practice simultaneously frees and offers power.

Spiritual knowledge is the process of passing from fear to a way of loving that is richer, more tolerant and relaxed. Emotional love can flower into true love in the measure that the initial fire of the emotions cools down and is substituted by a wiser and more mature perception. True love needs a fresh and renewing atmosphere, without fears.

When you feel full spiritually speaking, you feel flowing over with pleasure, happiness, wellbeing, and that state helps you to accept the other as they are, because from your wholeness you give and share and you don't need or expect anything from the other. While you need something that you want the other to satisfy, you will have expectations and the fear that those needs might not be satisfied, and you will get frustrated more easily. When you feel like a being of peace, a being of love, a tranquil being, a being that is spiritually full and satisfied, your relationship with others is a relationship of sharing on a level on which fear is not generated. You are not asking for or taking anything from the other. An elevated sharing of love, of happiness, of knowledge, of wisdom takes place, in which you do not generate a dependency on the other.

Attachments and dependencies, fears and insecurity, block our experience of love, of peace, serenity, freedom, happiness. When you have a feeling of love that takes you to a state of joy, to wholeness, and then you attach yourself to the object of your love, be it a person, or a property, automatically the feeling descends into fear: you fear to lose the object of your love and, instead of feeling wholeness and enjoyment, you feel fear. Over time, that attachment turns into a dependency, and your thoughts and feelings turn, to a great extent, in relation to it. Your thoughts are in function of what you depend on, so that there is not wholeness; rather you start to become inwardly empty: that is, your energy level goes down.

Love in its purest form is a spring that pours forth from the depths of being. It is a luminosity that the vigorous spirit, knower of itself, sends out in all directions.

Learn the art of loving, being free and allowing to be. Pure, true, love is an unconditional love that flows freely. Do not cling. Love does not cling, and if what you love is yours, it will return to you, and if it doesn't, it never was.

Moving from a Possessive Love to a Healing and Freeing Love

We live under the illusion that we can take happiness from objects, people and places, but happiness is something we experience when we put our heart into something, and our intention is of giving and not taking. In the creative activity where you feel most enjoyment, you will see that your happiness comes from within and expresses itself towards the outside, and not from the outside in.

Unconditional love is healing and never wounds. When you add attachment and dependency to love, that love will not be healing, because there will be expectations in it. When love is mixed with a desire for possession and attachment, you want to control the other and, from that control, exercise power over the other in order to have them in submission, influenced, because then you feel that you have them and that they belong to you. In this kind of relationship there is pain.

You are born as a free being. But when the people that love you begin to feel that they possess you, you do not feel free, but rather controlled. It is one thing for someone to look after you and care for you out of and for love. It is another very different thing for them to control and dominate you. To overcome the fear of loss associated with detachment, it is useful to nurture the truth that possession is a mirage. From a spiritual point of view, it is not possible to possess anything. Everything comes and it goes. Everything in life comes and then passes; it goes. To cling to anything is useless, a waste of time and energy. If we manage to realize this, we are very close to experiencing happiness, enjoyment and the joy of living.

If our heart is attached to something, depending on someone or something, it will be impossible to experience true enjoyment and happiness. When we are attached to something or someone, it means that our mind and heart are taken up by our attachments, making sure that "they are close" and often we lose ourselves in them. In this state of consciousness we cannot stay open to the new things that come into our lives: in fact, we are blocking them out. Preoccupied minds and closed hearts make it difficult to see and receive these new ideas, opportunities and even people, in our lives. In a true state of consciousness of the soul we are freed from the chains of attachment. When we recognize ourselves as spiritual beings, we can forget the many false concepts about being that have made up a part of our education and conditioning. In so doing, we lose nothing. On the contrary, we rediscover our real and authentic self. We are in charge of our inner world and access to our spiritual power.

Connect with Your Inner Mentor
If you can become the mentor that you would always have liked to have, then you will experience life as an exciting adventure.

What would happen if you had someone in your life that walked with you each step of your way, loved you unconditionally and supported you without putting conditions, even when you were wrong? What would happen if you felt absolutely safe, secure, cared for and loved? Would you be more willing to accept the challenge? Would you go for it? Would you take on your life with greater responsibility and wholeness?

Meditation: Discover Your Inner Mentor
Your internal mentor is a part of you and is always present, always kind, always loves you, is always there for you. If you still haven't met it, take a moment to guide yourself through this exercise:

1. Relax your body and allow yourself to be fully present, here, reading these words, listening to the sounds around you, feeling what you feel. Read slowly!
2. Now send love to each part of your body: your feet, your

buttocks, your lungs, your back, your face, your eyes, your nose, until you feel the love from your feet to your head.

3. Now send love to each thought that appears on the screen of your mind, visualise how your energy is concentrated at the inner part of the centre of your forehead. Try to make each thought that you generate full of the energy of love that is slowly invading you. Love what you yourself create: each thought.

4. That part of you that can give you love is your inner mentor. As you practice spending time with yourself in this way, you will start to see that your insecurity and your fears begin to disappear and new possibilities open up in front of you.

Suffering – Is it Unavoidable?

"My heart is afraid that it will have to suffer."
"Tell your heart that the fear of suffering is worse than the suffering itself".
Paulo Coelho, The Alchemist

In relationships, you sense that the other can hurt you. If you believe that the other person is wounding you because they do not meet your needs, how can you know if it is really the case? When there is a projection in relationships, it is difficult to realize it. Furthermore, does the belief that they are going to hurt you influence the situation until in the end it happens? Perhaps they won't hurt you. Your belief that the other is going to hurt you is not so powerful that it will necessarily affect the other person. But it affects you yourself. They may not hurt you at all, but you will end up hurt, you will become ill, you will become psychically ill. The symptoms will begin to show themselves and you will say: "Look, do you see? I feel hurt, I keep telling you so."

The other person isn't you. In relationships, when you project onto the other, a moment comes when you don't know if it is their fault or yours, if it is their responsibility or yours, if that person has brought on the irritation, or if it was you, if that person began the argument or it was you, if they generated the conflict or if it was you, because we project our energies onto each other. All of this drives us to frustration.

A lot of power, negative or positive, is needed for a person to be able to influence others with their consciousness. We don't manage to understand the dynamic of the human relationships onto which we are constantly projecting. We don't understand, and the reason is that we don't see ourselves, because we are always looking at the other, putting the responsibility onto them, blaming them, criticizing them. Looking at the other, sometimes positive emotions are generated and sometimes negative. On the one hand, love, wellbeing, happiness is generated on being with them; but then dependency, attachment and expectations are generated. We are afraid of what will happen. On always looking at the other person's behaviour, you stop seeing yourself and being aware of your reactions and taking the responsibility for generating your responses – that it is you doing this, not them. You get frustrated when the other person does not meet your expectations. As you depend on them, if they don't act as you would like, if they don't ring you at the time you would like or were expecting their call, if they don't do what you think they should do; this frustrates you. You project onto the other: "they are not doing what they should be doing," and so you feel frustrated. All the while that you hold the other one responsible for your frustration, you are not in charge of your own reactions, because you have given power to the other to dominate your emotional world. It is there that you lose your freedom. You lose your freedom because you give to the other, in the name of love, power over your own moods. You allow the other's energy to enter and generate in you frustration, bad moods, irritation, unhappiness and a mental and emotional dependence where you are constantly thinking about where they are, what they have to do, what they have to say, where they have to go, and all this consumes a lot of your mental energy. Wanting to control the other and the frustration that it brings with it uses up a lot of emotional energy.

The World Health Organisation reports that, in Europe, mental illnesses are the illnesses most on the increase. That suggests to us that our minds have become weaker. The intellect, the mind's eye that observes, is not strong in most people. The mind generates many thoughts, but the intellect has weakened, the capacity to see and understand the thoughts. The intellect has lost its capacity to exercise power over the choosing of one's own thoughts; for example, to distinguish a thought that is really going to take you in the direction that you want in order to achieve your life goals. The intellect is explored further in the chapter Getting Back Your Inner Power .

Some people seem to be almost addicted to pain and suffering and to being sad, crying (outwardly with tears or the silent cry of the heart and mind within), for themselves or for others. The reason that some people feed that state is that in some moment of their past, when they expressed pain, unhappiness, suffering, and illness, they were given love and attention. That is why they now use it as a tool of attraction, of union, of receiving attention and care. Sometimes it is used unconsciously or consciously for the opposite, as a tool of separation. A person can grieve as a natural healthy part of a process to get over the trauma of the loss of someone dear to them. But other times a person becomes sad as a method of isolating themselves and being able to say: "You don't understand me; you don't understand my life or my problems". Then you separate yourself from the sources that can help you. At the basis of this is the fact that you want to claim their attention, affection and help. But you isolate yourself in sadness and even depression, making it hard and even preventing yourself from taking that support, that help. In this way, your suffering increases. This process is a sign of the vicious circle you have fallen into, a sign of emotional immaturity. You go against yourself: you want help but you block the possibility of accepting it.

We are surrounded by a culture of grief in the world. There are even medicines to support and maintain this culture of suffering and to convince you that "you do need these things". There are counsellors and therapists that can convince you of those traumas or situations in your life. So you resort to various forms of grief and suffering, which return again to your consciousness and you relive them. The "patients" have created that suffering and that addiction. What they want is to convince themselves that they are right. That is why they need to have two or three counsellors, therapists, psychologists, at the same time to convince them that what they are feeling and perceiving is correct, and that they have to continue to suffer. They do not want to come out of it. Suffering can create addiction; it is the mental need that they have to continue to suffer. That is the culture of suffering.

Pain is like a messenger. It signals to us that once again we have our eyes closed in the face of our true spiritual nature. Pain, on any level, is no more than a wake-up call. However, instead of listening to the messenger, frequently we throw it off (in doing so denying that the problem exists) or we submerge ourselves in pain (with the belief that a little bit of pain is good). In reality, we often convince ourselves that pain and suffering are inevitable and even necessary. We have got used to the pain caused by fear and anxiety, and we are not aware of any harm in the occasional bursts of rage and anger.

Some of us are afraid of freeing ourselves of our anger because in a way it keeps us joined to the person that has hurt us. Anger is a form of intense attachment, like love, even if it is negative. Both forms of emotional intensity keep us connected to the other person, and that is why many couples who are legally divorced are not emotionally separated. If you cannot speak on the phone or be in the same room as your ex-partner without feeling your stomach clench, you are still attached. Detaching yourself can bring on a lot of anxiety, and it requires great courage. But once you achieve it, the liberation you receive opens you to many opportunities.

Sometimes we want to put on armour to protect us from the shame, anger, depression and anxiety that rejection can bring about. When we take a rejection as proof of our imperfections, we find it hard to risk showing ourselves as we really are again. The fear of rejection gets stronger when we start to think that we are inferior to others, or the image that we feel obliged to project. Rejection can lead us rapidly to the shame that we might have felt in our childhood. If you begin to feed ideas that you are boring and undesirable, it is possible that you will end up avoiding intimacy and that you will never allow yourself to be known. Or that you will place yourself on the defensive and reject people because you fear that when they see you as you really are they will think that you are not worth it. If we recognize that rejections are not a condemnation, but rather an experience that we should all face over and again, they will be easier for us to bear.

Those negative emotions are transformed into common features of the landscape of our daily life, and if someone suggests that it would be better to get rid of them, we reject the idea, since we are incapable of imagining life without our daily dose of negativity and adrenaline.

In some areas of psychology and personal development the theory exists that we should not repress our emotions, that "expressing them" is healthy. However, this only reinforces the *sanskara* [8] habit of creating our negative emotions.

The spiritual solution is not to allow such emotions to appear and to extract from the center of our consciousness, qualities of love, truth and peace, and to use them in thoughts and attitudes directed at the world that surrounds us.

If we are going to be conscious of the original nature of the self, it is not a question of repression, but rather the opposite: of us concentrating on our natural positive qualities and, simply, not giving space to the negative ones, and those will dissolve themselves along the way, in the measure that we express the positive ones.

Pleasure and Pain

There are two things that move us in life: pain and pleasure. Both create addiction. We feel pain in the body, and sometimes it is even emotional. But suffering arises in the mind. The suffering in the mind arises from thinking negatively towards the self, towards others, looking at them with a vision that consumes grief, sorrow and suffering.

Both extremes, pain and pleasure, can create addiction. On creating addiction it can start to form part of someone's identity. Later if one tries to stop the pain, it can almost feel like a threat towards the self, and towards one's own identity as one perceives it, given that suffering is identified with. It is too hard to see oneself as no longer suffering.

Years ago I gave a course of meditation to a mother in Segovia who had seven children. Her son had learned to meditate and became very happy and joyful. Seeing his happiness the mother came to learn to meditate. With a few sessions she felt much more at peace, but she told me that she was going to stop meditating and leave the course because she was starting to no longer feel afraid of what might happen to her children. The meditation was awakening in her a love free from fears, but it brought on in her an inner clash of beliefs. She believed that to love someone is to suffer about them.

We have the inner belief that love, worry, fear and suffering go together. It is difficult to transform fear until we eliminate that belief. You are love and you need to share that love. Life is a sharing of love, it is loving the body, loving oneself, loving others, loving God, loving nature, loving work. That energy of love in the end purifies us and helps us to go forward. But while the belief exists that love has to be linked to fear and suffering, we will be blocked and will brake the flow of pure love. In the name of love, we worry, we suffer and we are afraid. Instead of helping from a place of love in freedom, we help out of worry and fear, and in doing so we stifle, control, depend, and the other person feels their inner freedom restricted. We do not let them be.

If we review our personal history and see the moments when we have experienced most pain in our lives, we realize that it is with the people we have most loved, and that have most loved us that we have suffered most. We experience pain in a relationship of love, where there is possession, control, submission and dependence. Other times the pain is caused by a loss that generates an inner emptiness. That person filled me, they gave me wholeness, they were the reason for my existence and now they have gone. I wouldn't say that they "have died", but rather that they have gone to another level of existence. This idea is developed in the section on Death: Liberation or Loss? In the chapter on Fear of Illness and Death.

When there is too much pain we cannot lean back into our true power and experience our energy of love. The fear of love and the greatness of what you can achieve with its power prevents you from rising up to get it back. We fear our greatness and this fear keeps us in a restricted and painful state. Only the power of pure love, unconditional love or love of God, can help us to get rid of the repressed pain of the subconscious to the conscious conscience.

When you live through a situation that causes pain in you, you have to love yourself, stabilize yourself and enter the silence. Observe that pain without being afraid of it. Observe it to let go of it and understand what it is that it brings about in you.

The answer, generally, is connected with others: "He/she doesn't love me any more and that's why I feel pain", "Things are not like they were before", "The company doesn't produce the profits it was producing before".

If a person loved you and now has stopped loving you, does that make you feel pain?

Or is it your own expectation and your desire for that person to keep on valuing you or loving you like before that trap you in pain? Is it that you don't accept change?

The truth is, we bring on suffering ourselves. If you don't want to make yourself suffer, starting from now you do not have to endure any more suffering. Nobody can wound you, except if you allow it. So how do you allow it? By being a vacuum that sucks in everything of the other, the good and the bad, and you suffer. It is expectations that make us vulnerable to the experience of suffering.

Love does not stick to things; it liberates the past and unblocks energy.

Fill yourself with divine love, with peace, with silence, love yourself, and you will stop having so many expectations, and then your relationships will be conducted from a place of health, harmony, acceptance.

Open your heart and let the pain leave. Do not ask where it comes from. It has an old past. Embrace this pain so that it can leave. You do not need your pain. Let it go. Don't cling to it any more. Don't justify it. All you need is a true, sincere and loving heart.

It may help you if you practice Meditation 10: Letting Go of Pain.

If something makes you suffer, I suggest to you that you carry out a personal review. Go to the silence, revise your expectations, your desires, your projections and, in the silence, learn to let go. Don't keep a painful experience attached to you, let it go so that not only do you not keep it in the chambers of your heart, but also – now they sell those shredding machines – shred that experience and now not even a trace of it is left. That way you clean out the cupboards of the mind. Now you no longer accumulate more dust, more suffering, more pain or sorrow. What hurts us, much more than what happens to us, is giving our permission, our consent, to what happens to us. What wounds or hurts is not what happens to us but rather our response to what happens to us.

As Eleanor Roosevelt said: *"No one can hurt you without your consent"*.

And Mahatma Gandhi said: *"They cannot take our self-respect away from us if we do not allow them to"*.

Pain is the Messenger for Transformation

The paradox of pain is that in suffering there is a blessing, given that suffering becomes a stimulus for transformation. Whatever it is that reaches the self, it is simply a response or a reaction to what has come out of it. The normal state of the physical body is health. When there is illness, the feeling is of being unwell, of discomfort and of pain. Pain comes as a signal, to tell us that something has deviated from normality and that it requires your attention. Without the feeling of pain, perhaps you wouldn't realize that something isn't right. So, even when pain appears to cause suffering, the paradox is that it is acting in a compassionate way. Probably you wouldn't be stimulated to go to the dentist if you didn't feel the pain of a toothache. Thus, pain comes to prevent greater complications and so that you can repair or give immediate treatment to the damage.

Sometimes pain comes to warn us of danger. A child who puts his hands dangerously close to the fire might get burned if the pain brought on by the heat did not make him take his hands away quickly, thus remaining protected.

The same is applicable to emotional and spiritual levels. The "normal, healthy" state of the human soul or psyche is that of peace, love and joy. When you feel these qualities inside you and in the environment where you live and work, you find that you are happy, comfortable. In the moment that these joyous qualities do not exist, there is a feeling of discomfort, of unhappiness and you realize things are not as they should be.

In terms of physical pain, we medicate ourselves with herbs or remedies or we go to hospital. In terms of emotional pain, when the feeling of love and joy no longer exist, when your mind is uneasy, you need treatment.

Sometimes you think that this is part of human life and in this way you let it carry on naturally. However, in the same way that healthiness is the norm and is your right as an individual, emotional health is the right of each individual. It is your right and your natural state to be able to feel joy and love constantly. Having accepted this state as your natural state, if a feeling of suffering or pain exists, you should ask yourself why.

In terms of physical pain, you look for its cause. It may be the result of an external cause – a lesion, a wound, food that has upset your stomach – or something that is not working properly internally. In terms of emotional pain, the cause may be that something isn't well in the self, the psyche, or in your understanding of your relationships and the outside world. In both cases, physical and emotional pain, you look for someone to complain to or a guilty party, someone that isn't you. Some, in their distress, even blame God. In that state of awareness, you will not be tolerant, the most likely thing is that you are impatient and even aggressive, and the pain will become more intense and sharp. Another reaction is to be tolerant and accepting. In this state, pain is borne with a sense of responsibility and is contained, meaning that it does not have other repercussions. In the first case, there is a reaction, you have involved others and you have stirred up in them a lack of peace, unhappiness and anxiety. In the second, the calm is included which spreads and reaches others, relieving them.

Part of the skill of tolerating is that you see pain as training, as a process of learning that is taking place in you. Both physical pain and the emotional or mental kind teach you to increase your inner power and to detach yourself. In physical pain, the learning of detachment facilitates your letting go of the difficulty. In this training you ask the individual to focus on their source of living energy, which is felt as a point of light on the forehead. On doing this, it is as if the energy is concentrated and focussed, and from this source, you radiate rays of light and peace throughout the body. You will notice a great difference between the tension and pain of the body. After focussing your energy on the center of your forehead, there is a conscious detachment from the body, a feeling that the body is a separate entity from the source of living energy, and in this state there is not a great sensation of pain. With your mind you calm the pain.

In situations of difficult relationships or circumstances, the practice of detachment reduces the feelings of pain. One state is the state of being involved, whereby the emotional strings are tangled up and in the hands of the other. The other is that of a detached observer who has a clear perspective and can take the necessary steps in the right direction. Allowing suffering to remain and pain to grow brings bitterness and harm to the self, and it also makes your actions and reactions towards others wrong.

Another way to deal with emotional pain is to use the profound understanding of eternal truths in such a way that your attitude is transformed. Instead of reacting to situations and allowing the cycle of cause-effect to accelerate, that is, action-reaction, you can develop a state of non-reaction. Whatever the external cause is, if you confront it with stability and calm, you break the cycle of action and reaction. And you open up the possibility of adjusting the causes. You can drag up inner pain from the roots of the negativity of the inner self. Generally, it is difficult to accept responsibility; it seems much easier to place it onto external "guilty parties". If you use some time to reflect, going to the inside of your being, you will see that everything that comes to the self is the reaction and response to what has gone out of you. In silence, with detachment, without blame but with clarity, you will be able to see that in some situations it has been your ego that has been hurt and that is what is causing you pain. A mother can slap her child with anger and often she is the one who ends up crying with pain because of her own reaction. Attachment or possession creates ties and impositions towards others and they take away your own freedom, which causes you a profound pain.

Greed makes our desires multiply and, because of it, there can never be contentment but grief. First you should realize and accept the cause of your pain and then, you should generate the power of transformation.The paradox of pain is that if you hadn't suffered, probably you wouldn't have realized, and you wouldn't have the profound desire to change. So it is that the blessing of pain can lead you to transformation.

The union or connection with the Supreme through silence, meditation or contemplation, fills the psyche with its original and innate qualities and negativity is automatically dissipated. Another method to resolve pain consists of involving oneself in elevated, pure actions, serving or caring for others. Often this works instantaneously; one's own grief is forgotten on seeing and helping with the needs of others. The service that you give brings you blessings that lessen the grief.

We have been looking at physical and emotional pain, and through this we have seen the unhappiness of the self and of relationships, and the method to resolve it.

To a great extent, the paradox of pain also extends itself to the systems and structures of the world, such as the family, the economy, religion, politics and the environment, which are all in a state of profound pain to the point of disintegration. Again it is an indication that these systems are in need of an urgent re-evaluation and repair. They are all based on human values and in times where moral, ethical and spiritual values have collapsed. The systems no longer function as they should.

The pain in human life is a sign that our attention should be focused, once more, on the creation of a healthy structure based on the values of truth, love, purity and justice.

THE FEAR OF ILLNESS AND DEATH

The human being is psychosomatic by nature. Our health is profoundly influenced by our behaviour, thoughts, emotions and social relationships. Therefore, in order to care for our health we should care for our life style, our mental, sentimental, emotional and relational world, as well as our communication.

Fear is bad for our health. Manifested in the form of anger it promotes coronary diseases. Fear repressed for a long time ends up producing auto immune illnesses and degenerative disease such as cancer. As well as cancer and heart attacks, there are other illnesses brought on by fear: addictions, alcoholism, baldness, anxiety, arthritis, asthma, crying attacks, irritability, nervous breakdowns, back pains, diarrhoea, cystitis, sciatica, constipation, memory loss, gastritis, hypertension, menstrual problems, digestive problems, duodenal ulcers, vomiting, palpitations, impotence, and migraines.

When we get old, our neurons do not die, but rather the connections between them disappear. That is the conclusion of the recent research carried out by Michela Gallagher at the George Hopkins University. The neuronal connections or synapses keep us lively and young. When we have pleasant experiences, such as being surrounded by friends or working in a team where we feel happy, the neuronal connections are more fluid. However, the lights go out when we feel fear. It is an emotion that is capable of slowing down and blocking the electrical impulses between the neurons. With fear we are less creative and we get older more quickly. If we do not want to suffer illnesses (or get worse) we should learn to manage and overcome fear.

The fear in illness connected to the fear of death is the greatest fear the human being has. We are afraid of dying because we do not know what will happen during and after death. We do not know if God will be there to embrace us and take us towards the light or if in reality we will go to a hell or disappear completely and no longer exist. We do not know what will happen and we are afraid of the unknown. The fear of death can include the fear of pain, of letting go, of seeing yourself alone, of the unknown, and conversely the fear of transcending, of God.

Have you read or heard of near-death experiences? Just over two decades ago the first book was written about the subject of near-death experiences. Since then, many books have been written on this subject, with experiences of people who have been clinically dead and have then lived. One of the first was written by Dr Raymond Moody. He had seen how people with terminal illnesses died, and he also listened to the experiences of people who appeared to have died, but lived again. Their stories were a little strange, so he decided to research into it. He began with scepticism, but ended up by believing.

Dr Moody recorded the experiences of people who have been clinically dead and found a theme repeated in these near-death experiences. The situation that had led them to a state of coma was different: it may have been an accident, a critical illness, or something that happened in surgery, the heart stopped, was no longer beating, and they were 'clincially dead'. And then after five or ten minutes, in some cases even after 45 minutes, they returned to life and told a very similar story.

The story is that the body was here and they were separated from the body. For example, they were lying down in the operating room and it is as if they were above their body, on the ceiling, and could listen to and understand everything that the nurses and the doctors were saying and, on returning from the coma, they explained in complete detail what each one had said. Even if they hadn't died, if they had simply been anaesthetised, there was no way they could have had that information.

First they described the state of observer that they were in, observing everything. Then they passed on to a different experience, as if they were able to see the film of their life before them. They could see all their life passing and advancing very rapidly, and, then, it was as if they went through a tunnel of darkness and, at the end of the tunnel, they went towards the light.

Not the light of electricity. A light that seemed to have a personality, a light full of love, a love that accepted, unconditionally, that did not judge, that made them feel safe and protected. They felt an experience of euphoria and joy, and of immense freedom and unity. Finally, something happened and they came back again. Perhaps a doctor was resuscitating them, making their heart beat again, or perhaps they remembered their child, their husband or wife, and that memory brought them here again; for whatever reason, they returned and had that experience to tell of, but they returned transformed. They were no longer so interested in material gains, they returned with a different awareness and lifestyle. They came with love and compassion towards humanity. Above all, they returned with no fear at all of death. Thousands of these experiences have been recorded.

You do not have to go through an experience like that to understand that it is not necessary to be afraid of death, because, in fact, all the spiritual teachings tell us the same. All the spiritual traditions have spoken of how the soul is eternal and immortal, and we have been told that the body is dust and will return to dust. All tell us that we are children of the Creator and, as such, we are created in His image: we are divine energy. We have heard or read these things, but how are they experienced?

The practice of meditation, of contemplation, introversion and inner silence, facilitate for us the access to that experience of the immortality of the soul, the experience that the soul is eternal. Because in meditation we return to the consciousness of the eternity of being that I the self am, and the experience and awareness that I, the soul, am separate, I am distinct from this physical body. I recognize how valuable and precious it is: the body is the temple of the self, being, the soul, and living consciousness. But I realize that what I am is in my consciousness, in my soul.

What is most important? Think about it. It is not the color of your skin; it is not the color of your hair or your eyes, or the shape of your nose or your features. Your values, your personality, your consciousness, these things are important: your thoughts, feelings and emotions are not the body. You express them through the body, but they form part of your personality. All that is in the soul. The soul is eternal and immortal.

Meditation allows you to feel that you, the soul, are distinct from this body. And the soul can never die. You are the owner and master of this body, so you do not have to be afraid of dying. Even if you are afraid of death, the body will die. Fear doesn't prevent it from happening. I was reading about the experience of someone who said that they felt death to be very near. They had been threatened on a political level. They had lived with anguish all this time because they were in a situation of danger and they had seen themselves dead so many times in their mind, that eventually they realized that it was not worth being afraid of death. That anguish had taken away from them energy, vitality, preventing them from enjoying the present.

When we meditate, we access an experience of the immortality of being and of understanding that death is like one more step in the journey of life. It is not a question of believing it, but of experiencing it and feeling it, because if not, we will continue to have that fear. Those who live with the fear of death do not live well. One thing is to take precautions so that death does not come to us before time, and another is to live with the fear that death might come to us at any moment. With this fear we do not enjoy the present and we die many times before death comes to us.

From the moment that we are born, it is true that we will have to die some time and, when death comes to us, you cannot tell it "wait for five minutes". When it comes to you, it comes. The fear of death is the biggest existential fear that we have but it is a fear that arises out of a lack of knowledge about the experience of death and the eternity of being. However, there are many fears connected with the fear of death that cause us anguish for many seconds of our life. In the measure that we free ourselves of the fear of death, we also free ourselves of the fear of illness. There are many illnesses that we find difficult to heal and overcome, and fear doesn't help us, since it weakens our capacity to gather the necessary strength to deal with it and continue living. Surgeons tell us that a person who wants to live recovers better and more quickly from a heart operation. A brave person, with self-esteem, who is not afraid of illness, has a stronger immune system to overcome the illness or the operations more successfully.

Dying is like taking off the physical skin, the physical body, but that step only lasts a second. The physical energy changes, the body transforms itself; now it functions and, when it stops functioning, it will be transformed into ashes. But the soul, being, spiritual energy, doesn't die. I have explained the experience of people who have lived through a clinical death, but have then continued to be alive: they tell us of the experience of light, freedom and peace that they have felt in those moments. We are energy; each one of us is an energetic being. Life is energy. When life goes, the body does not have energy to move itself, this is called death. The energy goes from the body, the light goes, the dynamism goes. The energy that moves this hand is a mental energy that gives it the instruction to move; what happens is that we do it automatically. When we walk we don't say, "now I am moving my right leg, now my left leg, now the right, now the left", "now I breathe in, now I let the air go…" We don't think about it. We walk and breathe in an automatic way. It is our life energy that moves the body and our mental and feeling world.

Death: Liberation or Loss?

Sometimes we experience pain and suffering because of a death that leaves a great sense of loss. That person filled you, they gave you wholeness, they were the reason for your existence and now that person has died, they are no longer physically at your side. That is why loneliness invades you whereby you feel a great emptiness.

I believe in the immortality of the soul and, therefore, we can be in connection with loved ones. They have not died, they have gone on to another plane of existence. My brother lives far away from me, but I can have a connection with him. The other day I rang him and he said to me: "I was just thinking about you". What does this tell us? That there is a mental, telepathic and heart connection, even though physically we are neither speaking nor together. In the same way, when someone – their spirit, their soul, their consciousness, their life – leaves the physical plane, it transcends to another dimension, but we can feel its vibration and send them our thoughts and feelings. We can even feel their presence. For that person, if their body was in a bad way, the best you can wish for them is that they suffer no more. But out of selfishness you want them to stay here. If that person has to be kept alive with machines, with artificial apparatus and can no longer move, everything hurts them; the time has come for them to leave this physical dimension. But you cling on to them and out of selfishness, you don't help them in those difficult moments because you don't let them go in peace, you don't let go of them. Other times their death is not from the natural process of aging but rather an accident or sudden cause.

What comes in there is the understanding of karma and of the destiny.

In Dr Raymond Moody's book *Life After Life* people who have been clinically dead, then come back to life, talk about the experience and what was most difficult for them. At the moment that they felt they were entering into a tunnel of light and a liberating experience, the suffering of their family members or loved ones trapped them or slowed them down in that process and journey of liberation. They didn't allow them to go in peace. Is this love or attachment? Attachment. You tie the loved one down, you don't set them free. We have to help a person live fully in the here and now, and help them to die when their moment comes. Give them encouragement, energy, courage and the desire to live when there are hopes that they will recover. Love them in order to help them live and let them go in the process of the final journey. In this way our true love is strengthened, and we don't allow ourselves to be controlled by attachment, greed and selfishness, as this makes us feel pain.

During a publicity tour for my previous book *Who Rules in Your Life?* I toured the United States, where almost a third of the population is Spanish speaking, primarily from Latin America, and various lectures and events were organized in Spanish for me. I was staying in the home of an English woman who lives in Orlando. She had been married to a man of Indian origin and they had had a very fulfilling life as a couple. Her children were grown up and married, her husband had died suddenly five years before and she had fallen into great suffering. She felt an enormous emptiness; she wondered each day why it had happened, and each day as she lingered on it, her pain, sadness and grief increased. When she began to meditate, she changed her attitude and tried to give thanks that she had lived such a satisfying life for 40 years of her life. Her vision changed; she understood death from a more spiritual perspective. Instead of living lamenting her loss and complaining, she began to rebuild her life and to have an attitude of gratitude. Her life now is one of service and she helps many people. She changed the questions that her mind had been formulating every day. From asking herself: "Why did this happen to me?" "Why did he go when he was still young?"she moved on to ask herself: "What can I do from now on that might contribute something positive?" And she began to give thanks for all that she had shared and learned in those 40 years of life in a partnership. According to the questions that you ask yourself, the answers they generate can lead you to increase pain and suffering or to free yourself and be reborn in each moment.

Live Each Day As If It Were Your Last

Martin Luther King jr said: *"Nobody is truly free if they are afraid to die."*

If we are all going to die and we don't know when, then it only makes sense to live each moment fully. If we are all going to die and we don't even know when, then – what sense does it have to involve ourselves in activities that don't give rewards on the way and that only, perhaps, in the future will give us what we want? If we are going to die and we don't know exactly when it will happen, why not wake up, strengthen ourselves and fill ourselves with courage to live each instant with plenitude and with all our resources and inner values fully functioning?

In some way, all fears come from the fear of death. If you go step by step down the stairway of fears (and what would happen if what your fear takes place? What would happen if that fear became reality? etc.), you will inevitably find that you arrive at the fear of your own death. Being in peace with yourself each morning, thinking that perhaps today is your last day, you free yourself during the day to live fully. Every day enjoy yourself, learn enormously, free yourself and overcome the fear of fear itself.

"Live as if you were going to die tomorrow,
Learn as if you were going to live forever."
So said Mahatma Gandhi.

Each morning, on looking at yourself in the mirror, ask yourself: "If today was the last day of my life, would I want to do what I am about to do today?" If for several days in a row the answer has been "No" – it is a sign that you have to change something.

Remembering that you will soon be dead is a very good resource that can help you to take the important decisions and choices in your life. Many things, such as external expectations, all pride, all fear of shame, of being ridiculous, or of failure, fall away in the face of death, thus leaving what is truly important.

Remembering that you are going to die is one of the best ways to not remain trapped in thinking that perhaps you will lose something or perhaps you have something to lose. You are already naked. You came with nothing. You will go with nothing. There is no reason not to follow your heart.

In general, nobody wants to die. Even the people that want to go to heaven do not want to die in order to get there. However, death is the destiny that we all share. Nobody has escaped it. And that is how it should be. Death is one of life's best inventions. It is the agent of change in life. It clarifies and cleans up the old to give way to the new.

Now the new is you, but in a not far off future you will gradually get old, and the old will move on to give way to the new. The cycle continues. Life recycles itself continuously. Your time is limited. And thus your life is precious. Don't waste it living according to the life of the other, to their expectations, their impositions or opinions. Don't stay trapped. Don't allow the noise of other people's opinions to stifle your own inner voice. Have the courage to follow your heart and intuition. In some way you already know what you really want to become. The rest is secondary.

HEALING THE PAST

In order to be authentic, open, sincere and honest, you have to heal the past that has stayed recorded onto the heart of the self. Heal it so that your heart can love without fear, and all your being can show itself without hiding, without bitterness or rigidity.

To overcome fears, it is necessary that your mind is not weighed down by the past nor worried about the future. It is important that you are at peace with your past.

Revise your past; if there is some part of the past where you feel bitterness, repentance, hate, fear or unhappiness, it is good to cleanse it. You can have bad experiences, but learn not to record them in your memory. With inner strength and with mental power, that is, with a mind that does not repeat the weak, the negative, and does not keep on thinking about bad experiences, you can deal with situations and live through them with flexibility, lightness, tolerance and transformation. If in your consciousness there remains a minimal impression of something of the past, some experience with someone, when you look at and speak to people you will do it with that attitude and vision. That impression of the past will prevent you from seeing things with the clarity with which to observe the present moment with clarity and without prejudices.

Thoughts create a world and, when, besides, we speak about something, we widen it or make it bigger on putting it into words. Thoughts about the past are old thoughts, which create an atmosphere of this kind, and that influences our interactions and relationships.

Your weak and useless thoughts create vibrations that produce a useless and wasteful atmosphere. It is important to finish with even old vibrations.

If you generate pure, positive and renewing vibrations, with the power of these vibrations you can put an end to useless thoughts. Cultivate healthy, beautiful and powerful thoughts. These thoughts carry such energy that, definitively, they will put an end to useless thoughts. Begin by cleaning up your thoughts. Then strengthen and generate the power of purity and authenticity in your thoughts; that way you will create thoughts that shine, and are sincere and full of meaning.

Accepting

The healthy attitude you should have in the face of your past is to accept it fully and to be at peace with yourself and others. If this means to ask forgiveness, if it means to clear things up in any way, or if it means to do the work of transforming a negative experience into positive, it is worth trying to do so. If there is not full acceptance of the past, you will live unhappily and it will lead you to become frustrated, get depressed, fall apart or simply be in a bad mood and have mood swings that are difficult to control.

Reconciliation with Things You Have Lived Through

Some fears arise due to the situations we have lived through; for example, if you are driving a car and you have an accident. Then you take some time to drive again, because the memory of the accident awakens the fear of having another one or reliving the one you had. The person that has never had a car accident gets in the car with confidence, because they do not have that scene recorded, since they haven't lived through it.

Obviously, there are fears that we carry within us that are not of the present. Something happened to us in the dark and we are afraid of the dark. Fears in relationships: you opened your heart, you fell in love and, after a time, you experienced pain. They got you here, they got you there and you felt hurt, misunderstood, manipulated, deceived or mistreated, and now you no longer open your heart for anything; it is closed off with the shields that you yourself have created. To overcome this kind of fear due to experiences you have lived through, you have to reconcile yourself with your past and accept it fully. You cannot change your past; lamenting the past doesn't help you; complaining about the past doesn't benefit you. Those shields brought about by fears do not disappear unless you do a profound cleansing. Begin to heal your experience of the past. Part of the past is healed with forgiveness. Without forgiving, you cannot forget.

The work with oneself to see what aspects of your past weigh on you and clarifying yourself with your past, requires silence, reflection and meditation. When you reconcile yourself with your own past, you can let go of it and be free of it, not be afraid that that past will come back to you. If not, sometimes, it is like a shadow that follows you.

If they robbed you, the shadow follows you that, perhaps, they might rob you again.

If they hurt you, you fear it will happen again. Sometimes that experience presents itself in dreams, in the subconscious or in present attitudes. Reliving the past in your mind, you do not fully enjoy the present. You have to accept the pieces of your past so that they do not continue to generate upsets. Accept that you had to live through them and live the present with a constructive vision of the future.

I find it helps me to write letters to God about my experiences. The exercise of sharing them with God in writing brings clarity to me and helps me to bring the divine light to my life in order not to be weighed down by unnecessary experiences, unhappiness or grief. Have you ever written to God? I usually do it at night and I tell Him the things that affected me or that I have learned. I tell Him the things or intimate feelings that other people perhaps wouldn't understand or wouldn't be there to listen to. I also talk to Him about all that I question. And the following morning, when I meditate and study early, I often receive answers.

Cleansing the Memory

To clean the files that are stored in your mind, you need to make a constant effort in the purification of the self. If you generate positive thoughts, you can change the direction of your thoughts; and if you are having a useless or negative thought, if you pay attention, you can redirect your thoughts. However, cleansing the self is not only done on a mental level. Redirecting thought by channelling it in a positive direction is not enough to cleanse and change the habits that arise from what is recorded on the memory, from the experiences you have lived through. They are memories that are recorded there. All that has generated some tendencies towards fear, depression, phobias or developing various habits that weaken you as a person.

To gain access to that inner world you need to feel, visualize, live yourself as free of all that weight. It is like being born again. My experience in the 30 years that I have been practicing meditation and working on all these matters is that I have been born again many times. When one is born it is as if the blackboard were empty, clean, and there is an enthusiasm and renewing energy that burst forth from within.

Although we arrive in the world with a set of characteristics, with the different experiences you have from childhood onwards a series of impressions are recorded on your memory and on your inner register that lead you to be more violent or to be afraid or to get depressed; or, the opposite, to feel a security and trust in your capacity for success and to have good communicative skills. All this is recorded over the years, with the education we receive and with the different experiences that we live through. However, we can be reborn: recycle, transform, improve and be.

Be reborn – what am I referring to? Everything that you have accumulated you recycle. I will give a physical example: at home, sometimes you accumulate things that you think you might come to need, but after a time you realize that you haven't used it and that it is of no use to you. It bothers you because it takes up space, accumulates dust and you don't need it; then you give it away, or throw it away or recycle it. In the same way, we go along accumulating things in our being that we do not need; they take up space in us, they are a weight and a bother and they make us unhappy by causing bad habits.

So in the same way that from time to time you should do a clear-out of old things, you also have to clean out your inside, since, if you don't, you carry an emotional and mental weight that leads you to have unnecessary phobias and fears. They make you feel the insecurity that you might fail again, that you might have that accident again and that you might live through that experience that frightened you again. On getting rid of them, you leave a space for the new: it is a rebirth.

With the practice of meditation you learn to decide what experiences and habits you want to continue in your life and which ones you want to get rid of. It is important to think positively to maintain good self-esteem, trying to choose and fix scenes, dialogues and other positive memories of your patrimony of memories: feeling loved, having been successful, having enjoyed yourself. Learning to clean out certain inner registers and strengthen others is a sign of having a full capacity of self-management.

In meditation, in reflection and in the silence, you learn to reconnect with your cabin of inner controls, which includes:

- Thought.
- The capacity to discern.
- The capacity to decide.
- The capacity to make a judgement.
- The capacity of what is useful to you and what is not.
- What you want and what you don't.
- Everything recorded in the store of your memory: your memories.

In that store of what you lived through it is very possible that there are many things that are the seeds and the causes of many fears that you still retain: perhaps you felt wounded, deceived, you were taken advantage of, you were rejected, this happened to you, that happened to you, you failed, you were ill, you had an accident. Clean out your store and burn the old and useless files. To clean out files that are dirty, weak, that hold bitterness, grief, anger or other painful experiences inside you, you have to:

- Be ready and prepared for the change it means. It might mean the death of a part of your being, of your ego, of your attachment, and the rebirth of the authenticity of your freer and more brilliant self.
- Be prepared to let go and to do some work of profound introspection.
- Some files have to be forgotten, some erased and others destroyed through burning.

With time you have filed away experiences that from time to time emerge, influenced by a situation or at a given moment someone touches something in you that "opens" that file. To clean it out and for it to disappear, you have to burn it. Burning old experiences that bring about unhappiness and weakness means healing yourself profoundly. On the one hand, you have to accept, forgive and forget. On the other, you have to fill yourself with the power of silence, the power of divine love, the love of God, and allow this to purify you.

Forgiving and Forgetting
When I was in El Salvador some years ago, I gave a lecture in which I said: "If you do not forgive, you cannot forget".

Then a lady came to see me, so grateful! It was some years since someone in the guerrilla war of El Salvador had killed her son. She had spent many years with so much bitterness inside her and with an inner violence of wanting to make "him" pay, the one who had killed her son, that she was not living in peace. That bitterness did not resolve the situation, the only thing it did was increase her pain. She understood that she hadn't forgiven and because of that could not forget.

Many times we keep bitterness in our soul because we haven't forgiven. Sometimes, when it is a question of a broken relationship, it is not only a matter of forgiving the other, but of forgiving yourself for having allowed yourself to enter that experience. It was you that took the step to allow that experience to be entered into. If you hadn't taken that step, you wouldn't have had that experience. You accepted that challenge, that relationship, and what might happen in it.

So not only do you have to learn to forgive the other, but also to forgive yourself.

Sometimes, someone says something in three minutes that makes you feel really bad –they said it in three minutes but it is still there a month later. How could they! Who do they think they are! Something happened in three minutes and you remember it, you repeat it again in your mind and in your words, and you recreate it. With this you strengthen that experience in your register, so that after two years you remember what they said to you. The other person unburdened themselves and forgot it straightaway. It's like the person who takes out the rubbish, throws it away and forgets about it. Someone throws four words at you and they forget, but not only do you not forget but you repeat them in your mind to such a point that at times it doesn't even let you sleep. Learn to forget memories that generate shadows, pain or fears in your present.

The past has already gone and what you have now is the present moment.

Clarifying

On other occasions forgetting is not a question of forgiveness, but of clarification. The person is alive and you simply have to say a few things to them in a good way, in a conversation, or by letter, email or phone. You want to communicate something to them and the fact of repressing it accumulates inside you and, if you don't communicate it, you will explode. That repression brings an increase in unhappiness and pain in you.

Clarify what you feel, express yourself out of peace and good feelings.

Look for the right moment to be listened to as you deserve.

Sometimes we "let go" what we feel at a moment when the other is on another wavelength, doing another thing or occupation. Then we get frustrated because we are not listened to. When we want to be listened to, we have to create the atmosphere, seek the moment and make the other see that what we are going to say is important for us.

Turning Over the Page

It is very positive to learn to put a full stop and turn the page. That has already happened. It is past. To achieve it, a great mental power is required. When you have it and when you practice it in your life, you feel a mental lightness whereby you do not go along accumulating things that are not good for you and you only allow what you consider to be valid to be recorded.

Many times, the mind lives more in the past than in the present, or it has fears of the future; those worries turn into fears about what might happen, and you feel insecurity and fear about the future. By riding between the past and the future the mind cultivates fears of things that you have lived through or fears that perhaps you might have to.

It is important to learn to cleanse the register of your memory. This is possible, firstly, by learning not to accumulate certain experiences in the register of your consciousness, of your memory. To do this, practice the statement: "What has happened is over, it has already happened". What happened this morning already happened. You don't need to recreate it in your mind, turning it over and over, or think about it so many times, because that strengthens in your mind the experience of what happened. It is past.

Do not let your mind re-live what is useless.
Value your time. Value your creation: your thoughts.

It is a practice that you can begin to do from now on. For example, if there has been an argument, you argued; that's it, it is over. Don't go back to it, to have another go. If you do so, you exhaust yourself. You don't resolve the situation or the relationship. Sometimes an argument is like a monologue where nobody listens to anybody; one listens to oneself and doesn't hear the other. Put a full stop and that's that. Don't allow your mind to stay stuck thinking about it over and over again. If you find it hard to control your mind, focus on your breathing to bring your focus to the present.

The body acts as a resonance box that indicates to you your emotional and mental state. The tensions, the blockages, the rigidity of the body and other symptoms warn you that something is not flowing in your life. Yoga helps you to be aware of what is happening inside you. Doing yoga makes it easier for you to live in the present with maximum wholeness, dissolving the resistances that prevent you from accepting things as they are.

It is not difficult. Right now you can stop for a moment and observe your posture. Is there tension in any part of your body? Relax it. Concentrate on that part of your body that is tense and, conscious of your breathing, on doing so you send energy to that tense part and you relax it. Sometimes you are tense out of habit and a lack of attention. Centring yourself on maintaining a good relaxed posture helps you to avoid back problems and to be present in your body in a conscious way.

Yoga helps you to connect with your inner space and awaken your positive energy. This makes it easy for you to find a solution to what is bothering you and to change your attitude. Keep your inner space clean of fears, complaints and resistances. Free yourself of that negative energy and enjoy the moment.

To clean out all that is useless that has accumulated within you, begin by concentrating on your breathing and totally accepting your body. The different postures that yoga offers help you to enter into a state of silence and harmony of wholeness. In each posture flexibility is generated, the blockages are dissolved and you live that experience of reconnection with yourself; the mind stops digressing and you are centred. You enter into an experience of silence, in harmony with your body: relaxed, flexible and aware of your breathing, you learn to take enjoyment from your inner space.

Asking Yourself Appreciative Questions

Go with care about what you ask yourself about your past. There are questions that stimulate and awaken pain; they increase it and make you unhappy. For example: "Why have I had to live through this?" "Why has this happened to me?" "What did I do to deserve this?" "How is it possible that this had to happen?" What kind of answers do these questions generate in your mind? Rejection, hate, bitterness, aggressiveness; you become irritable, bitter. You re-live your past and you re-live it badly.

Instead you can ask yourself other kinds of question such as: "What did I learn from this situation?" "What can I improve on so as not to live through it again?" "What is it that this situation is asking of me?"

This kind of appreciative question generates positive answers, answers that lead you to love, generosity, forgiveness, to tolerance and learning.

Visualise Yourself Free of Influences

There are visualization techniques that help you to see yourself as a shining being, free of past or present influences. Each one of us has our perfection. Instead of seeing yourself with the vision of the past, learn to see yourself as you will be tomorrow. See how you are originally, who you really are, a free being; a being without fear; a being of peace; a being full of values and virtues; a being of love; a divine being; peaceful, elevated, spiritual energy; a strong being, healthy and full of life.

You are life.

Invoke this positive vision and bring it to the present. In you are rooted values, virtues and powers. A value that contains spiritual and divine energy becomes a virtue, and that contains the power of God, which turns into a power. When you have the value of love, but also its virtue and power, that love is unbreakable; it is altru-istic; it is indestructible; it is true; it is authentic. With visualization you see yourself in that state and, with that vision, that state emerges from you. Instead of seeing yourself as you were yesterday, a frustrated person, with fears and in submission to the influence of others, you see how you can be tomorrow. This technique is one of the bases of success in personal and relational transformation. Visualizing like that helps us to be reborn. For more guidance, and practice, see the section Visualize in the chapter on Meditation.

Letting Go
In your consciousness you have a store cupboard where you accumulate everything that you have lived through. It has files of childhood, files of your relationships and of different experiences. Some contain bad experiences and pain. The heart may be hurt, broken or wounded. You carry it with you. What do you do with this past? What has the past done with you? The past is already passed, the situation has passed. Letting go of it is the best way to erase the pain that there is in your soul and that has left furrows on your brain and your heart.

Meditation helps not only to heal the soul, but that also, physi-cally, the impact that experiences of pain have left on your body is erased. This happens with the practice of deep meditation. Not with a relaxation of a few minutes or with a superficial meditation.

The experience of deep meditation will help you to completely heal your soul of fears, pains, and accumulated sorrows.

On letting go of the baggage of the past, the fears that you have in the present, brought on by previous experiences, will disappear. Simply let go of it, don't question it, and don't re-live that situation in your mind even one more time. Let go of it, it already happened, you had to live through it. That's it. Now you are at a specific date, today, and that happened in 1998, in 2000, or in 2002 or yesterday, whenever. It happened. Let it go, let it go; don't cling to it any more. It is greed, bitterness, anger, fear, attachment and dependence that make you cling on.

How do you trap a monkey? You give it a bottle with a neck wide enough for its hand to fit and inside the bottle you put peanuts inside. The monkey puts its hand in the bottle, takes the peanuts and cannot get it out, because its hand is full. And it doesn't let go. You have got it. The only thing the monkey has to do is let go of the peanuts and take its hand out, but it doesn't let go! That is how we are at times, like monkeys, we don't let go and we remain trapped into situations, people, and the past. And for the sake of a few peanuts! Really, it is not worth clinging on and feeling the suffering and pain that it brings on, when we could avoid it.

Be wise. Let go of what extinguishes you. Let all those accumulated experiences that make you feel pain, bitterness, hate, fear and unhappiness, go.

It is important to be at peace with your past to fully enjoy the present. Clean out the influences of your past that reduce the potential of your being.

Don't allow negative situations or those that do not help you to leave a trace on your being. Forgive, don't hold resentment or fear that the situation will repeat itself. Don't question or relive that situation in your mind, Let it go, it already happened. Accept that you had to live through it. Full stop to the past. Live in the now.

Be calm and don't speak of yesterday. Today is beautiful. [9]

GETTING BACK YOUR INNER POWER

Self-conquest is the highest victory.
Buddha

To reach, savour, and maintain a state of wholeness you have to know how to use the freedom that capacitates you and permits you to achieve the full realization of your individual self, to have faith in this freedom, this wholeness and have faith in life. You have to know what brings you close to this state and what distances you from it. Fears are one of the main enemies that act as an obstacle to opening yourself to wholeness.

Any weakness, inconsistency, dispersion, lack of focus and inner fluctuation will steal from you the energy that is necessary to feel whole. You should take positive risks in order to concede yourself power. Free yourself of any aspect that throws a shadow over you and allow your being to manifest itself and express itself with all its potential.

To live in wholeness you should be in charge of your inner world.

If not, you will only be able to experience temporary moments of wholeness.

To achieve wholeness you not only have to have inner control but also to revise whether there is any crack or door open to weakness in your personality. Because if you strengthen yourself on the one hand and on the other you are weakened, you will never reach that state of inner power.

If you fill a bucket of water but it has holes or cracks, however much water you pour into the bucket, it will carry on emptying itself. In the same way, this can happen to you. Because of this, you have to find out which are the holes and cracks of your personality through which there are leaks of energy, which mean your efforts will not have the results you hope for. As much as you try to fill yourself, the emptiness generated by these losses will continue.

Getting back your inner power means recognizing:
- That you are responsible for how you are.
- That you have a potential in you to discover and develop.
- That you need to have greater control over your inner world, resources and faculties, your mind, intellect, traits, conditioning and habits.
- That you should strengthen values such as tolerance, acceptance and flexibility if you want to live peacefully and survive the times of turbulence and change we are living through.
- That there are beliefs and habits that bring about in you fears, doubts and suffering that you could avoid and be happier.
- That there are beliefs that block you that you should change.

Fundamentally, we do not take on the responsibility for our own life. It is easier for us to blame others for how we are. When you are irritated you think that it is because this person is like that or acts in a certain way; or you are in a bad mood because the weather is like it is; because the house has a crack in the ceiling; because the builder hasn't come; because the car won't start; because you have twisted your foot; because of this, because of that... So you are always complaining and frustrated. But who is responsible for that frustration? The car, the builder, the house, the ground that was slippery, or are you responsible for what you do and how you respond to what happens?

Stop being the victim and take on full responsibility for your own reactions.

This is the initial base for getting back your inner power.

You have spent years with a mind that thinks a lot, thinks unnecessarily, with habits that are not altogether healthy. Transforming all this requires interest, will, perseverance, study, practice and above all, patience. The results will come.

To get back that state of personal control that gives you the capacity to love without depending, to love and be free, to love without being afraid and to live without fear, you have to revise your beliefs. Do you believe that to love you need to worry yourself obsessively? Do you believe that worries are healthy, help you to channel the energy of your mind to find solutions? If the answer is no, then revise why you hold on to these worries. In conserving them you do not make good use of your life energy. One of the main energies is the energy of thought.

The human being is made up of the human, the physical, corporeal, and being, which is spiritual. The mind forms part of being and has an extensive function, given that it thinks, imagines, desires, creates, associates, remembers, projects.

You will find that you are one way or another according to how you use your mind.

We are all the creators of our own thoughts.

Clarity of Mind

People are just as happy as they make up their minds to be.
Abraham Lincoln

To strengthen yourself you need to have mental clarity. It is convenient if there not is not so much excessive thought as to generate clouds, unhappiness, suffering, grief, indecision, doubts and negativity – thoughts that your mind produces and that are weak, useless or wasteful. All of this clouds your own clarity. You should do inner cleansing. Think less, think concretely, concentrate, think in an elevated way, and your thought will have an energy of clarity and inner strength that will help you to put it into practice with greater success.

You should strengthen yourself to achieve a state of self-control. To strengthen the self, you need self-esteem, clarity and self-control. For this, you need to study yourself, know yourself and understand yourself. You need inner silence, for there not to be so much mental chatter from thinking, thinking, thinking and thinking.

On top of that, other people influence you and so you generate even more thoughts. There are so many influences and inner voices that speak to you. With all of that there cannot be clarity. There is the voice of your fears, of your ego, that of desires and greed, there are influences of the past, thoughts emerging from your values, your neighbors', your children's, your husband's or wife's influence, your mother's or father's, the influence of your work colleague's opinion, or the psychologist, the life coach, the trainer, the consultant, the massage therapist. You can listen to many inner and outer voices and, if you are not strong, your mind weakens under so many influences, which has repercussions on your clarity of mind. Because of all of this you have to strengthen your mind, which means, think less; think slower, concentrated and clear thought; with sense and meaning; of quality, based on a healthy and positive motivation. That thought is like an arrow: it has positive strength and clarity.

Sometimes you think, "I am going to do this," but then another thought comes, another and another, and hours go by... "Oh, but I was going to do that and I haven't done it!" "I was going to call someone and I haven't called".

The thought came into your mind but – why didn't you do it? Because you were not focussed; there was neither clarity nor focus; there were so many other thoughts and distractions, one after the other. Then you go from one task to another and leave things half done, unfinished. Your list of what still needs to be done becomes endless, and disorder, lack of organization, increases in your life. When you do something without being sure of what you want to do, doubting as to whether you should do it, fearing failure if you do it, and doubting as to whether you will be successful, whatever you do; with all that doubt, you will not have much force. However, when you do something basing yourself a clear vision, a state of self-esteem, on your values, of trust, serenity and wellbeing, with that clarity, concentration and focus, you will be more successful, you will be more conclusive and you will have the capacity to carry it out. On approaching things in this way, you will feel satisfied.

The capacity to understand how you think and feel and where your thoughts and feelings come from is very important. Without that understanding you cannot rule over your own inner kingdom, which is made up of your mind, your heart, your intellect, your memory and beliefs and habits. Your mind goes one way, your heart another, and there is no union, harmony or balance in your inner world. There is a clash of voices, conflict between them and confusion. Sometimes you channel your thoughts in a way that is harmful for you, and only you are responsible for this.

You also have to understand that what you see, hear and feel generates thoughts and feelings. It is important to understand and realize that you have the capacity to decide how to respond to what you see and what you hear, so that your responses are not impulsive reactions that unbalance you internally. You have to pay attention to what you think: you have to be alert and attentive. It will only happen if you are connected to your most authentic and deepest self. You need to be connected not only to the outer layers of your identity, to the body, to your role, and what you have to do, but to your *inner* awareness, to the depth of your being, to what you really are and your soul wants.

In the origin of each thought there is a belief, a value, a vision or a perception of reality and it is there that you have to do that deep and spiritual work in order to know yourself in more depth and transform what is necessary. That requires the disciplining of your mind. If you know that something is not good for you and you decide that it really doesn't benefit you, then why do you carry on with it? Out of habit, custom, weakness, dependence or even addiction. If that habit is harmful to you – why do you carry on doing it? Each action that you do generates an imprint on your store of memories and memory and generates and feeds the habit. Every time that you do an action based on that habit, you strengthen it. If there are habits that are harmful to you, transform them. One habit that reduces happiness and tranquillity is that of thinking that things are going to go badly: "It's not going to work out for me" "It's going to go wrong". There are people who constantly expect the worst and before it happens, for better or worse, they are already unhappy. If you expect the worst, how are you going to feel?

The future is uncertain, you don't know what is going to happen; the unforeseen can always arise however much you plan. The mind is always projecting the worst onto the future, onto others and onto oneself. With these thoughts you will be anxious, frustrated and fearful, because you expect the worst and you are afraid that it might really happen. What you have is the present moment; instead of enjoying it, you are expecting the worst, with thoughts like: "He won't come" "What if he has had an accident?" He hasn't called, something must have happened to him" or "They are going to fail me". What benefit do you gain from this habit of expecting the worst? Does it benefit you? So, why do you keep on with it? Who creates your thoughts? Who expects the worst? You do. Why do you create them if they are no good to you? They harm you. Have power over yourself and put your useless and debilitating ways of thinking into order.

What thinks, feels and keeps memories is the energy of the conscious being. When you learn to purify and clean out your capacity to think, you strengthen your capacity to think positively, to change the direction of your negative thoughts that generate fear, worry and anxiety. When you clean the intellect of fears, your capacity to reason, discern and decide, improves. When you are responsible, honest, sincere and true with yourself, you learn to have a cycle of thoughts that is healthier, more meaningful, higher and of quality.You need clarity, discernment, decision, concentration and determination. With these powers you will be the owner of your life and you will feel more satisfied, full and happy.

The vibration and content of the thought can go from the most physical to the most spiritual with intermediate states: emotional, mental and intellectual. As a human being, you can express yourself from a lower state than that of animals, that is, a state whereby not even your instinct works. Animals have an awakened instinct. For example, when the Tsunami in Asia took place, the animals in Thailand went three kilometres inland from the coast, into the forest, because their instincts made them feel that something was happening, that they should protect themselves and should go inland. Thanks to their awakened instinct they protected themselves in time and saved themselves.

As human beings, at times we do not have an awakened instinct. Other times we function with that instinct, which is distinct from intuition, which is divine.

Instinct is a faculty or instinct that you have to defend yourself: run if something happens or get out of the way so as not to be burnt. We can function by basing ourselves on the instinct. It is on other levels: emotional, mental, intellectual or spiritual, where the intuition is awake and in tune. More on intuition later.

Your thoughts can be ideological or intellectual; your thoughts can be materialistic, vulgar, ordinary, mediocre or negative; or your thinking can be full of quality, content, spiritual, divine, unlimited, sublime. Who does it depend on? On you yourself.

With your thoughts you can even reach the point of creating or freeing yourself from pain, even though the body feels it; with spiritual thought you don't suffer so much from that physical pain. You are capable of going beyond the experience of suffering, with the thoughts that vibrate on a healthier, higher, more authentic and spiritual level. When you learn to generate those thoughts, your energy flows better, and in that flowing of your energy you are unblocked and feel that your communication is healthier, without complexes or fears. You are not afraid of expressing your true self, because you have nothing to hide, you shine and are yourself.

On the other hand, if you focus on having good thoughts, saying good words and carrying out good actions, you are not afraid. Negative thoughts bring about fear.

If you have thoughts of attachment, you will be afraid of losing the objects of your attachment, or obsessed with acquiring more. If you are attached to some shoes, to a coat or a bag, you will be afraid of losing them and of not having others. How many pairs of shoes can you wear at the same time? How many do you really need? When you begin to understand, you realize that negative thoughts are destructive. Useless thoughts cause fear. Nothing has happened, but you are worried: "Maybe this will happen". The idea that something might happen leads you to anxiety and fear. You have negative, useless thoughts, and your heart fills with fear. If you have bad thoughts and bad feelings, you are going to have a bad reaction; if you have good thoughts, you have a positive reaction. If you follow this principle of having good thoughts, saying good words and doing good actions, you will not be afraid and good will come to your life.

Spirituality teaches you to change the quality of your thoughts.

Mahatma Gandhi was once asked: "How do you behave towards your enemies?"

His answer was: "I see them as friends."

The Intellect

The mind, in these times, in most people, is controlled by their experience of the past, by their habits and by external stimuli. The internal capacity to control the mind, that comes from the intellect, is weakened. The intellect has the function of discerning, of judging the thoughts and deciding which ones to put into practice. But when the intellect is not agile, thought becomes action without that filter of discerning and deciding with clarity and determination. The intellect has become weakened, confused, atrophied or even, petrified. That filter of the intellect is nourished by beliefs.

The beliefs that we have today are connected to our cultural, physical, political, sporting, identity, or our mortal, corporeal identity, associated with our age, sex, of our body. Beliefs connected to materialism, to having rather than being, are living based on the perception of the senses, and not on intuition and the wisdom of the spirit.

There are beliefs that block you, or brake you, others break you, they bring about fears in you and a limited perception of reality and of yourself. However much you try to generate positive thoughts, if you do not change these beliefs, their influence will be so strong that the positive thinking will not have the strength or consistency to prevail.

The intellect is the faculty of being that judges thought and determines its quality, its ethical purity, its veracity, its usefulness, if it is appropriate, necessary, correct or incorrect. The conscience expresses itself through the intellect. The intellect determines whether a thought should become action or not.

If you have a positive thought, the intellect should support it and allow it to be put into practice. If a feeling of doubt accompanies the positive thought, the intellect should take it into account and erase that doubt. An inner conflict does not exist when the faculties of the mind and intellect are pure, clean, unflapping and have recovered their original function: so they are strong, and cooperate in harmony; they support one another.

If the intellect is weak, the mind feels confused or is fragmented; the energy of the mind will generate many unproductive thoughts. There will be an inner conflict and in the end the intellect will lose. Then, the intellect will not have the power to prevent them from going into action. Actions will be taken that are negative or unproductive, in opposition to the conscience, and they will generate negative habits.

The intellect is the most important faculty of human consciousness to attract change. Your sense of identity depends on the power and clarity of the intellect. This determines the capacity and quality of the intellectual processes through which you decipher and live out reality. If the intellect is clean and pure, you will distinguish truth from falsity rapidly and clearly, what is real and authentic from what is unreal and false. You can establish if a situation is beneficial or wasteful, useful or useless, true or false.

Not all that glitters is gold. Life presents you with many mirages that set off desires to achieve something unnecessary for your wholeness, or mirages that make you believe that you will gain something from a situation or person, without being true. Thus, you waste time going down a road that only leads you to disappointment; you waste the resource of your thoughts and you wear yourself out emotionally.

If the intellect is polluted, you make erroneous evaluations. Thus, you will make erroneous choices, dishonest or illogical decisions. You will justify dishonesty, you will accept erroneous contributions and you will be incapable of distinguishing between the real and the imaginary.

When your intellect doubts, your thoughts are confused and you will be indecisive, confused, careless, permissive, you lose control and are easily deceived.

A person with a pure, clear and clean intellect will act with honesty and sincerity.

When your intellect is polluted, you may act against your own conscience or against your better judgement; you may be insensitive. A person with a vague and doubtful intellect will justify a dishonest act. The process of purifying and cleaning the intellect is also a process of inner awakening that strengthens your conscience.

Being awake means to realize, and being strong means to act according to what you have realized. An intellect awoken to spiritual intelligence is the basis with which to trust and use attuned intuition, live with the pure, innate wisdom of consciousness.

Meditation Strengthens, Clarifies and Purifies the Intellect

Many people lament the fact that their intellect is not as clear as they would like. One of the aims of meditation and spiritual knowledge is to make the intellect strong, clear, clean and keep a sense of what is right, and maintain good ordering of functioning. Meditation allows you to develop the clarity of your intellect.

One of the effects of meditation consists of bringing about realizations whereby you realize what is happening within you. Sometimes we use the expression "He/she doesn't know what he/she is doing", referring to someone who is acting in an immoral or amoral way. Being aware and awake to the implication and the consequences of your actions is the best deterrent to not acting in an inappropriate way.

The voice of the conscience brings with it that state of "awakening" and "realizing". Because in meditation you feel quiet and you focus your thoughts inwards; in that state, the sound of the voice of the conscience is perceived. It is a voice that is not affected by material worries or a preoccupation about one's image and public appearance. You are not distracted by activities, noise, unrelated ideas, mental chatter and everything that separates you from your true self. In this way you can listen to yourself within.

Identity and Belonging

The deepest reason for the lack of peace and the abundance of rage, fear and lack of trust, whether it is in personal experience or in human relationships, is centered on the loss of awareness of our authentic identity and the true nature of our being.

Our identity is based on the physical (body), actions (what we do for a living, and the roles we play), possessions (what we accumulate), location (where we come from socially and geographically) and our conditioning (acquired beliefs). Basing your self-esteem on any of these things can become a problem, because all of these qualities are not permanent. When we base our identity on some of those factors, our life is spent on internal and external conflicts, defending and protecting one of the many false identities. Fear becomes our companion (be it the fear of loss or of pain). This is the essence and the universal reason for all suffering, lack of trust and conflict in the world.

We are in a society that promotes consumption based on an awareness that is totally corporeal: having more, the cult of the body and possessions. The result, which arises out of the belief that we are a body and nothing more, causes illnesses such as anorexia; it produces incredible expenditure on products with vain claims, and on vain and harmful procedures such as on cosmetic and plastic surgery. According to UN statistics, of the three industries that move most money in the world, one is the cosmetic. Another is the arms industry. That indicates to us our priorities on a world level. We fight against old age, when, in reality, fighting against old age shouldn't cost money, because it is a question of having a mental attitude open to learning and change, an attitude without fear, a flexible attitude, an attitude that is internally free, which allows us to reach old age active and young in spirit.

If you feel stable in your spiritual identity, conscious of it, not only have you overcome your fears but also you can eliminate the fears of others.

Some years ago, there was an earthquake in Athens, Greece. One of our meditation teachers from the Brahma Kumaris centre in Athens, shared an interesting experience after the earthquake. The earthquake happened in the afternoon. She worked in a publisher's where there were fifteen people working in an open-plan office. Everyone was at their desks working and when the earthquake began, fear and panic was unleashed. As a meditator, she remained totally calm. She felt intuitively that, instead of running, she should keep quiet and tranquil, and that is what she did. The people around her sensed her vibrations and, instead of starting to run, as prisoners of panic, they decided to sit down quietly. Her calm and peace created the atmosphere of calm and peace around her. She eliminated fear and they were all safe. When an earthquake or a situation of that kind happens, often the fear and panic cause more harm than the situation in itself. When we replace fear and panic with an understanding of ourselves, it benefits us and others. Fear is the origin of many of our weaknesses. Out of fear we put up defences and we hide behind an arrogant and proud image. Generally, the people who seem very strong because of their arrogance, their haughtiness and pride, are hiding their fears beneath those defences of the ego. A person who is not afraid does not have to prove anything and is very humble; they do not generate conflict or violence and nobody fears them. They can be a friend to others because they know themselves and know that no one can take what is most important away from them; that is, their own peace, their own happiness, their capacity to love.

When you control your mind, you strengthen the intellect and clean the register of your memory of all that is stored in the past; when you do those three things, you learn not to be afraid and not to have to justify, defend or prove anything. The sun does not have to show that it is full of light. The sun simply continues shining and giving light.

Each one of us has an authentic, original and true identity of being. We also have a whole set of "layers" that we have gone along creating and accumulating over time and that we have identified with. They make up a part of the creation of the ego, of the false self. Some of our identities are connected to the body: sex, if you are man or woman, if you are old or young, what race or culture you belong to, the colour of your skin.

Then there is the identity that is connected to social class, the education you received, the profession and position you have. All these identities change and, in reality, each human being, be they South African, North American, Chinese, Japanese, Indian, Spanish, Catalan, Basque or French; old or young; rich or poor; they have a spiritual identity. It is the identity that joins us to human beings.

We are thinking beings, conscious beings, who experience love, peace, happiness, respect, cooperation, tolerance, solidarity, all universal values that transcend that more limited identity of the body, of gender, of social class, culture or race that we belong to. That spiritual identity is not physical. A being, be it in a young or old body, black or white, can experience love and fear. They are experiences that the soul has, the conscious being, which is not physical, although they are experienced and manifested through the body. The body acts as a fuse box of the soul and warns us when things are not going well in our heart and inner self. Listening to your body helps you to listen to your soul. On listening to your soul you understand what your body needs and you learn to keep the organs and senses at peace.

Thought is an energy that has a great power. However, you cannot touch it physically. Thought influences the physical. If you have a thought of fear, your breathing automatically changes, and if you have a thought of relaxation or happiness, your body posture and breathing improve. That is the power of thought over the body, although the thought that arises from our conscious being is an energy that is not physical.

Transforming fears is a question of transforming on a profound level the vision that you have of yourself and your own identity. "Who am I?" Whilst you identify with the I that is limited, egotistical, only connected with the corporeal and the physical, that physical identification generates in you a limited vision of yourself, which leads you to relate to others in a more needy way. The motto of many people is: I want, I need; you want and you need; you want this and you need that. It is a relationship of dependence and of wanting to take. You forget your capacity and your mission to give and you only worry about what you can get and take from here and there.

The energy of our being, of our life, is made to share all of its beauty, that is to **give**. But when you disconnect from your own true self, from your own spiritual self, you begin to need to fill yourself from the outside.

When you forget that you are peace, you look for peace in nature, in others, in work or in professional satisfaction. When you are internally dissatisfied, you feel an emptiness, a state of personal insecurity and you need others to appreciate you in order to love yourself, others to tell you how well you are doing something, to feel that you are doing it well; that is, you need the positive projection of others towards you. That positive projection is felt as part of belonging. Unless a person feels that they belong to something or someone, unless their life possesses some meaning and direction, they will feel like a particle of dust that belongs to nobody or nowhere. They will not be capable of relating to some system that gives meaning and direction to their life, they will be full of doubts, and those, over time, will come to paralyse their capacity to act.

Out of the need for belonging, one identifies with a clan, a religion, a profession, family, with a community or a group, and all that gives security to the individual; they belong, they are rooted in a structured totality within which they possess a place that nobody argues with. That identification helps them to overcome the doubt and feeling of complete aloneness. However, it is also the cause of fears and conflicts due to the dependences and expectations it generates. During the day we are connected: with our desires, with people, with time, with events, with work, with action. But what happens to the connection with our true being? Why do we always live at the mercy of the currents, the waves and the wind? We don't know how to dive into the depths, find the treasures – our qualities, our virtues – and find thus the meaning and sacred element in our life: awakening what is authentic and truly valid, valuable and meaningful.

With meditation you learn to think about yourself, not selfishly, but rather strengthening your values, your true and original authenticity and identity. What is that identity? Who are you really? You should find out for yourself.

In silence and in meditation you learn to get back your state of peace, tranquillity, honesty and authenticity. You reconnect with your true being and thus connect with humanity on a spiritual and caring level. The conscience is awakened and the feeling of being a citizen of the world: you belong to the world and the world belongs to you.

You feel humanity as a brotherhood: we are all brothers and sisters in this great universal family, children of God, Father and Mother.

Personal Governance
When thought goes in one direction and feeling goes in another, it generates confusion and an unstable inner state. You generate insecurity and unhappiness. You feel one thing, think another and, in the end, don't know where to focus your energy. Having balance between thought and feeling means that there is inner harmony

and a state of wellbeing. Not in a state of battle between your mind and your heart, but of help, understanding and co-operation. To do so, you have to listen to your inner voice, the voice of your intuition, of your conscience, of your soul.

When your mind is constantly thinking, the majority of your thoughts are useless, superficial or connected to aspects of daily life – what you are going to eat; if you will go on foot, by bus or on the underground; what time you have the meeting, and so on.

A mind busy with thoughts directed at action does not help you to listen to your heart. They are thoughts that do not have a deep meaning, although they are necessary for action and the co-ordination of what you are going to do in your day-to-day life.

With the practice of silence you will be able to calm down the speed of your thoughts and listen to your heart. The power of silence takes you beyond all the limited attractions and any physical possession or property. To reach wholeness, a complete and perfect state, it is necessary to recover the power of silence.

With the power of silence it is easy to govern over the organs of the physical senses and over the subtle powers of the awareness made up of the mind, the intellect and imprints or features that are habitual parts of the personality (sanskaras).

The fact of being able to make any thought or aspect of your personality emerge at the desired moment allows you to overcome the subtle powers, this being the state of inner governance. In the same way as you give the order to any physical organ to do this or that, lift up your hand and the hand lifts up, lower the arm and the arm lowers, in the same way your thoughts, habits and the power to decide, that is, the intellect, have to work by responding to your orders. A yogi can keep his physical organs, his body, calm. There is no nervousness, tension or blockages or excitement. The bodily energy is in total serenity and harmony. When your conscience, the being that governs, gives the order to the mind, the power of the thought so that it stabilizes and concentrates instantaneously, its stabilzsing with only a thought is a sign that you are in charge of your inner domain. If your mind obeys after some minutes or, instead of stabilizing and concentrating, it becomes agitated and goes from one place to another, you are not in charge of your inner world.

It is important to know that you have the right over these faculties or subtle powers, that your mind obeys you instantly and only manifests the habitual trait you decide on. If you base yourself on this practice, you will achieve the dominion of your inner world.

To have governance is also to have a right over your own intellect, over your capacity to decide. To be able to make a decision in the instant that the situation requires, in accordance with the situation of that moment is being in charge of your own intellect. You should not feel that it shouldn't have happened, that it would have been much better if you had decided it before, or if you had done something different, when the situation or moment has already passed. Therefore, being capable of making the right decision at that time is a sign that you have governance over your own inner kingdom.

Each day you can review your subtle powers and see if your physical organs and your faculties continue to be under your control or not.

The original *sanskaras* – the innate ones – are made up of love, peace, happiness, purity and truth. They are good, the personification of all the virtues. They do not have random outbursts of fears, anger or other weaknesses. To achieve wholeness, feel yourself to be full and in line with your objective, you need those natural *sanskaras* to emerge and to act basing yourself on those values.

The Loss and Recovery of Personal Energy

If a light bulb is connected to a battery and left permanently on without being recharged, gradually the light becomes dim and eventually fades away completely. Only the bulb is seen. In a similar way, the soul expresses and emits its energy through the actions of the mind and the body. Mike George, writing *In the Light of Meditation*, says that the light of our consciousness, the qualities of joy and love and serenity, slowly diminishes over time. The only difference is that the inner darkness, which will eventually pervade our consciousness, comes not so much from the running down of the battery of spirit, but more from being swathed in the gradual accumulation of experiences and impressions, the influences of other people and from the world around us.

There is always light and power emanating from within the human soul, but it is diminished in both intensity and purity by this gradual gathering of physical experiences which leave layers of impressions and memories enfolded one within the other, like the petals of a rose that has not yet flowered. Thus, the person loses their sense of spiritual identity, and clear perception weakens gradually, since our original purity as beings of spirit has absorbed many impurities.

We only have to observe our inner self at this moment and see the inter-relationships and connections of our own mind, intellect and behavior to realize our present lack of personal dominion and the diminishing of our spiritual capacities.

Looking within and seeing the relationship between your mind, intellect and *sanskaras* is essential if you have to heal the spiritual scars of identification collected over many lives and get back your true spiritual awareness.

Meditation is the method to see and understand your individuality in a kind way, and accept your spiritual identity. From this understanding and acceptance you will get your personal energy back again. But you need to charge yourself up every day by connecting in silence with the pure essence of your being, given that in acting and doing we usually lose energy and allow ourselves to be influenced by the outside.

Creating a Wealth of Positive Thoughts

Positive thinking arises out of respect for yourself. Self-respect implies that you are conscious of the essential truth of yourself and you know on a profound level that any negativity that there is inside you is acquired and does not form a part of your original, innate and authentic state.

The mind tends to jump from one place to another. Thinking positively means to generate a wealth of positive thoughts that attract a positive inner experience.

Be conscious of the fact that you are the creator of your thoughts and feelings.

You choose how you respond. Strengthen your creative capacity of response.

When you do not have faith in your own capacity to resist pressure or difficulties, you feel insecure. A thought can block your capacity to feel whole, full, realized. Only a thought makes you sad or irritates you. A single thought can be the key to open the door that allows you to enjoy and feel the values of being. It has to be a thought that is pure, potent, clear and concentrated.

To create these kinds of thoughts that allow you to respond with creativity and not allow people or situations to take away your inner wellbeing, you can practice meditation and focus on these affirmations:

- *I am the essence of beauty.*
- *I am a soul in peace.*
- *I strengthen my being.*
- *I have the highest purpose.*
- *God is always with me.*
- *I am brave and stable.*
- *I deal with each challenge as it arises.*
- *I am loving and not attached.*
- *I am free to be happy.*
- *I am in charge of myself.*
- *I am authentic and live my own life.*
- *I am light, I do not carry burdens.*
- *I am friendly and sincere.*
- *I have a clean conscience.*
- *I respect my intuition.*

• *I have the right to success.*

Exercise – Creating Positive Thoughts:

To generate a wealth of positive thoughts, it is good to select the theme from amongst these affirmations of self-respect or create your own affirmation.

Be creative and generate a list of thoughts associated with your chosen affirmation of self-respect. Perhaps it will help you to write your own list. Consider your list and hold the feelings or associated images in your mind. Keep yourself attentive, centred and alert. If you lose the thought or you are distracted, bring it back to your consciousness again. Be aware of what is going on in your mind. Actively distance yourself from the useless, dull and negative thoughts that may arise to distract you. Focus on your affirmation until you experience the positive meaning. Be firm and stable in that state of self-respect. Cultivate your faith and trust in this area of self-respect by practicing these affirmations daily.

Value your inner world.

Think less, think more positively, think from clarity and silence. Strengthen, love and respect your being. This way you will develop the capacity to free yourself of the internal and external influences that make you small, act as shadows over you and extinguish you. Strengthen your self-esteem and learn to govern your habits and inner energies. Remember your value and use your positive qualities in action.

CHANGING HABITS

We do not take long to create a habit. We only have to think about something a few times and put it into practice, and that way it becomes an automatic thought and action. The thought that preceded the first action was still conscious. But the more we repeat the action, the less conscious we are of the thought that creates it.

A moment comes when we no longer know why we are doing what we are doing; it has become a habit. We are not constantly conscious of this information, but when some event or person causes certain feelings, emotions or desires to arise, it reminds us of those experiences of the past that brought about the habit.

In our society, the number of addictions and addicts is growing rapidly. It seems that human beings can become addicted to anything: credit card spending, eating, drinking, sweets, chocolate, tobacco, sex, relationships, watching television, surfing the internet, watching football, earning money, power, work, arguing, war. This demonstrates the existence of an inner emptiness that people try to fill with external things. To the extent that a human being becomes addicted to any of these aspects, their free will becomes weakened. If you don't realize it and put a brake on it, you fall into a spiral of automatic and compulsive actions that start to limit the freedom to decide what you want for your life, causing a loss of self-esteem and a state of depression, anxiety and dependence.

The origin of many addictions comes about due to a desperate need to flee from a situation, to solve a problem or from a spiritual need, whether it be a lack of respect, love, affection, care, attention and consideration, or lack of peace and inner serenity.

To overcome the addiction, attachment and habit, we need to go to the root of the problem and to be willing to change. Without preparing ourselves for change, we will struggle to overcome those habits of addiction, attachment and dependence. There are habits that are not pleasant and that harm our relationships. For example, when someone is frustrated, irritated, nervous or in a bad mood, it is neither pleasant nor comfortable being by their side. They complain all the time and generate a tense atmosphere. We are used to complaining and getting frustrated. We think that situations should be how we think they should be, people should act as we think they should, and we too, and, as none of the three things always works as we would like or as we think they should, we get frustrated, irritated and end up disappointed. When you justify your frustration and your complaints, it is difficult to transform them. It is an internal psychological mechanism that is deeply rooted, so that transformation is more difficult. You don't recognize that your complaining attitude in the face of the situation won't improve it. You don't recognize that you are a participant in the situation. By complaining, your mind gets tired and you use your energy to make the problem bigger or exaggerate it, instead of looking for creative and effective solutions.

Generate the attitude and habit of accepting others as they are, and situations as they arise. Stop wanting to control everything. Control what you think. That way, instead of living in the culture of complaint and blame, you will start to create and live a culture of gratitude. The reality is that situations will not always be as you want them to be. It is in your hands whether your mental state is more stable and stronger than the situations, or the other way round, whether the situations determine your mental state and provoke your reactions. Remember: you are the owner of your mind and creator of what you think and how you respond. See the chapter on Control and Power.

Some think that to change habits you have to leave them bit by bit. I don't agree. When I saw clearly how important and beneficial it was to be a vegetarian, I decided on it one day and the next day I was completely vegetarian. A family member of mine smoked quite a lot and one day said to us: "From today on I am not going to smoke any more". And he didn't smoke another cigarette. You spend three or four days not feeling so good, but then the body gets used to it and that's that.

It is a question of being firm in your thought and determined in the action. If you see clearly that you have to do something, don't postpone it, don't let the excuses that your mind makes control you. Be firm, and with determination, you will see that it is easier than you thought. For example, if you have the habit of getting upset, angry and in a bad mood, do you dare to commit yourself to no longer getting angry, from today on? Because what use is it to get angry? Firstly, you waste a lot of energy, you exhaust yourself, you lose your own sense of peace and what's more, you upset those around you; then you have to fix the harm you have done to others with your bursts of anger.

What happens is that we lack courage and we do not dare take this kind of determination, because we don't control our inner world, we don't know ourselves nor are we aware of all the potential that we have within. We are more concerned about controlling our child or a loved one than controlling our own emotions, feelings and our mind. That way we waste and lose a great amount of mental and emotional energy without getting the results we are after. You can use mental energy for your health, to generate a good atmosphere at home, in family and work surroundings. Having good mental energy will help you to lengthen your life. To change a habit you need a lot of mental and spiritual energy. With a good disposition and a positive attitude, you live better in the present and the future: things start to be clarified and in their rightful place.

Being Ready to Change

We have to know the beliefs that implanted our habits and the attitudes that sustain them. Only then will we be able to change certain habits from their roots.

It is possible to change harmful habits. What would the methods be? Do we have to go to therapy, a counsellor, a psychologist? In my experience of dealing with many people I have seen a person change in seconds a habit that they had had their entire life.

And I have seen people who have habits that don't seem very harmful or problematic, but, although they want to eliminate them, they can't. I have seen people who smoked or had a phobia about something change a few minutes after someone has worked with them. The shared characteristic of those people is that they were ready, they were in the right place in their lives for this change to occur. Consciously or subconsciously, they were ready to take a step forward, to accept the responsibility for the creation of a change and to apply a solution.

It is not just about desiring a change, you also need knowledge in order to make the change. You need knowledge about what has been causing the creation and maintaining of the habit. When you realize that you have been creating this experience for yourself in your own mind and you understand that you have been the creator, then you can also become the destroyer by recreating a new vision, that is positive and self-affirming.

If the person is not ready and goes to seek help, they can even create an addiction with the therapist. They become dependent. A good therapist will prepare them to be ready to take the step or jump necessary in their life to change and be autonomous.

Use Your Energy for Change
"Use your energy for change." So says Mike George in his book *In the Light of Meditation.*

At the core of the soul there is a pure, spiritual energy of peace, love, truth and happiness which is not co-dependent. Awareness and experience of this energy provide us with the inner strength needed to change. Meditation is the method to access and allow this energy to come to the surface of our consciousness and into our minds to colour our thoughts and feelings. In much the same way as hot, molten lava flows from the core of the earth to the surface through a volcano, we can create volcanoes of power when we meditate. We want to use our energy in a positive way; we are not seeking the kind of power that manipulates and causes damage.

When we experience our own source of inner peace, we essentially become free of any dependency on external sources and substances for feelings of contentment and calm.

When we generate our own feelings of love and self-acceptance, we cease to be dependent on others and our addiction to their acceptance and approval diminishes and eventually disappears. When we generate our own feelings of contentment within ourselves, we become free from the need for substances, places or physical experiences in order to be happy.

Using this inner power in the right way allows us to let the old addictive habits within our personality atrophy and eventually die. Any unwanted habit can be changed and the scars of all the negative habits, which have developed within the soul over a long period of time, can be healed.

A Positive Vision of Being

It is much more important what you think of yourself than what others think of you.
Seneca

When a person falls in love, the marvellous thing about that falling in love is that it is a totally positive projection. There is a person who projects on to you all that is positive: you are marvellous, you are unique, you are indispensable, you are a treasure. That positive projection generates a euphoric state, of bliss, of wellbeing, whereby you are flying. You feel loved, cared for, needed and valued. That positive projection lasts for a time until, with the dependences and expectations, the negative projection begins. "You should have called me, you should have told me, you should have come, you should be more like this, you should be less like that, you should have done this or that."

With these expectations, demands and dependences, that positive projection and idyllic state disappear. You are interfering in the other's space and the harmony is lost.

You should learn to have a positive vision of yourself. You are marvellous, you are unique; don't depend on them telling you so. This does not mean you need to feed your ego, but that you need to make the most positive emerge from within you. Resort to all your creative, positive, spiritual capacity, so that you do not depend on others having to project positive things onto you in order to feel good. On feeling good in an independent and autonomous way, you will be able to share with others peace, love and positivism. You won't be in the state of victim whereby others will say, "Oh, the poor thing!" Why do you want to be in that state of victim? What's more, the person complains more, to generate more reactions like that. Why do we want to generate that response? What is wrong with us? Why are we not the leaders of our own lives? Why do we have to be, or try to be, the victims of others and get frustrated with them?

What would happen if you had someone at your side that walked with you every step of your way, loved you unconditionally and supported you without minding what happened, even when you were wrong? What would happen if you felt absolutely safe, secure, cared for and loved? Would you be more prepared to accept the challenge? Would you go for it? Would you take on life with greater responsibility and plenitude? Your inner mentor is a part of you and is always present, always kind, always loves you, is always there for you. See the section on Connect with Your Inner Mentor.

Discipline

All the religions and spiritual groups place an emphasis on a certain discipline. Without discipline you do not manage to transform negative habits and you do not create a new state of awareness where the self is nourished through the experience of spirituality.

Every day you have breakfast, you eat, have dinner, drink, breathe, and all of this you do not consider a discipline; you have adopted them as something natural in order for your body to continue working. On a spiritual level you also need to nourish yourself and to have a discipline that, with practice, a time comes when it becomes natural because you incorporate it into your life.

In the process of change you need to discipline yourself in order not to let old habits come to the fore. Until you have "burnt" them and they have "died", you should keep the guardian of attention alert in order to maintain your self-control, given that each time you use a habit in action, you strengthen it. When you do not use it, you allow it to die.

You should be disciplined in order to maintain and realize your aims. In any area of human life, results are achieved and excellence is reached with effort and discipline. This applies to studies, sport, the company, art and any other profession.

Discipline is necessary for growth and personal transformation if you want to obtain satisfying and permanent results. If not, the old habits continue to rule in your life.

"The path of the awakening spirit is therefore one of waking (awareness of self as soul) and sleeping (under the illusion that we are our body), waking and sleeping. We tend to fluctuate between the two (like dawn and dusk) until we find stability in soul-consciousness. This is why it is important to awaken and stay awake, and why it's important to give our mind and intellect good spiritual food and exercise every day to keep them fresh and alert.

Being conscious of the soul, acting from that consciousness, the scars (habits and tendencies) left by past actions based on illusions of corporeal awareness are healed. The evidence that our discipline in the practice of meditation is working is a lightness of spirit and an increasing easiness in our interactions with others."

Mike George, In the Light of Meditation

LIVING THE VALUES

Change of Paradigm

If you try to prune a sick tree by cutting off some leaves or branches, you won't achieve anything. If the tree is sick and you only prune some branches or take off some leaves, the illness in that tree will continue. What you have to do is look at the roots and, when you see what is not working, you will see what you have to do with the tree's illness.

It is the roots that have to be cured. When you observe the tree of humanity and all the illnesses that are flooding our society today, you realize that, if you try to paper over the cracks of the different problems, here and there, in the long-term it is not a solution that is going to work. But if you look at the root of society's problems, you will see that everything has become very artificial and materialistic.

Instead of recognizing our spiritual identity, we think of ourselves as matter, and we connect our identity and our attention to the matter. As a result there is an enormous amount of fear. In the culture of fear and violence, as people we act basing ourselves on our ego, greed, attachment, anger, lust, laziness and arrogance.

If we want to change this entire situation, the answer is very simple, and it is the only answer: **change the paradigm**. Distance ourselves from the materialistic paradigm and enter a spiritual paradigm. Returning to a spiritual paradigm, we return to the values that are at the base of our civilisation and we return to the truth, peace and trust.

It is not governments that will bring about this change, not the religious, spiritual or political leaders who will bring about this change. Who can do it? You and I. In fact, each person has to do it for themselves. I cannot do it for you. I can only do it for myself. When a person changes, their change has an impact around them.

Returning to a spiritual consciousness is your responsibility. When you do so, you see that your world changes and you begin to live the kind of life that you could and should live: awakened, full, aware and responsible.

What Values?

When we speak of values, we should ask ourselves what they are and what their relationship is to the world and human life. Values are like the sea, unlimited, deep, rich in variety and colours, and they offer a dynamism of relationship and contact. As such, they break with routine and help us to act in a more creative, positive and enriched way. In this way, we can do without the standard recipes and instructions, since often they do not fit either our reality or what we are proposing. A value is the reasoned and firm experience that something is good or bad and that it is more or less good for us. These convictions organize themselves in our consciousness in the form of beliefs and scales of reference (scales of values). [10]

A part of society is concerned to integrate everybody into a certain system of values where what is most important is the cult of the body, of power, of individualism, of egotistical wellbeing, of materialism. All of them have to be questioned, given that they do not contribute quality or offer the possibility of a sustainable lifestyle.

In the face of this we should consider the necessity of promoting the true human values. Values are like models, guides or paths that mark the guidelines of an integral behaviour. Values allow us to find meaning to what we do, to take responsibility for our acts, make decisions with serenity and coherence, resolve personal, family and human relationship problems and define the objectives of our own lives with clarity.

The scale of values of each person will be what determines, at the end of the day, their thoughts and behavior. It is necessary to know who you are, what end you seek, what means will lead you to achieve that clearly defined life project and whether the objectives that you have set out for yourself are going to complete your self-realization and are going to provide you with peace, happiness and make you feel good with yourself and with others.

Authentic values help us to know ourselves, to love ourselves and, at the same time, to understand and love others.

Values give meaning to our life and facilitate a mature and balanced relationship with the environment, with our world and with people, occurrences and things in an integrated way, giving us balance and peace. The lack of a system of values will place people in a lack of definition and doubt. A lifestyle whereby you live in the integrity of values protects you, and you are not afraid of the uncertainty of the future. You trust yourself and in your capacity to generate wealth, friendship and wellbeing.

If you use your time and your resources well, you generate a good karma, a good destiny. What are the resources? Your body, your breathing, your mind, your money, your time, your skills, your qualities, your personal characteristics, your values. If you use your mind uselessly, waste your money, you waste time and waste your resources. What will be your achievements and how will you reach the wholeness of being?

We need to be coherent in how we use our resources so that nature will collaborate with us. Now, on a global level we exploit nature out of greed and selfishness, without respect, and at the moment of need, nature will not collaborate with us.

Let us use our mind well and it will collaborate with us. Let us use our body well, giving it what it needs, what it really needs. The person who says, "I need a cigarette" believes they have a need that, in fact, is unnecessary. Your body does not need to be a living chimney. You do not need to smoke. That is your attachment, the desire of your mind, your habit, your dependence and your laziness in the face of change.

You should strengthen the feelings that are based on your values, such as the feelings of love, trust, peace, happiness, being content, satisfied in feeling consoled and free. Those feelings lead you to a state of wholeness, since they generate an inner harmony whereby thought and feeling find harmony by basing themselves on those values. Take care that the thoughts and feelings that block that experience that leads you to wholeness, like fears and insecurities, do not interfere.

It is important to understand what values and feelings lead you to wholeness and what feelings block it. Wholeness is a state in which there is a total harmony in your being: spiritual, mental, of feeling and physical; there exists a balance between what you think and what you feel; there is integrity between thought, word and action. That is the state of wholeness, where there is coherence in your life.

The question is to strengthen yourself to direct yourself towards wholeness. Each human being, fundamentally, wants to reach a state of wholeness, a state where their life has meaning and significance; where what they do is worth it and, therefore, they love life and what they do. A state of wholeness is a state where you feel love, creativity is not blocked and the soul overflows with serenity. There is not worry or unhappiness.

Is it possible to reach that state of wholeness in the world of today, which we all have problems dealing with? Yes, it is possible, but it is a challenge; that is, we need to strengthen that part of our being that helps us to overcome problems with agility, to not be drowned in the problems.

As the Indian poet and philosopher Tagore [11] said, when he defined life as a river and the human being as the boat that flows on the river. When the river gets into the boat, this latter sinks. When the situations of life get into your being, you sink.

Life is a river.
You are the boat that flows on the river.
If you let the water of life
Get into your boat,
You will sink in the river.
Tagore

Your thoughts and your feelings are of anxiety, asphyxia, depression, because you have let the situations of life get into your life, that is, that situations influence you to such a point that you no longer control your boat, and it sinks in the situations of life. The more attached you are and the more dependences you have, the easier it is for you to make this happen. Dependence opens you to accept the influence of the object you depend on, whether it be a person, a property, a pet or an idea. Don't allow the situations that take place around you to sink you, to enter into your life in such a way that they absorb you, diminish you and slowly destroy your potential to shine and to be yourself.

On occasions you want to help someone and you ask yourself: How can I help my friend or this family member who is depressed? If you don't want to help yourself, like the example in the chapter on Suffering, of the woman who wanted to carry on suffering for her children, it is difficult for anyone else to help you.

When someone does not want to help themselves and is not prepared to make the effort to come out of that state, the way in which we can help is to be like a sun, to shine and give off light. If someone wants to take the light, let them open their windows and take the light and, if not, they will continue to be closed away in the house in the dark. But even then they know that outside there is light.

The best way to help is to free yourself of negativity, blockages and inner fears, and that way you generate an environment in which people are not afraid, they feel themselves unblocked and natural with you, they relax and feel comfortable with you. In that environment their most positive part can emerge, their inner leader, their inner ruler.

It is the best way to help your fellow man, being yourself, not humouring them because at bottom you want something from them, but rather loving them, allowing them to open themselves to their true being. Generating bridges and not walls.

To build more bridges and fewer walls you need:

To trust. Learn to trust because trusting yourself, others and life opens you up to unimaginable possibilities. Don't worry if someone deceives you, if the other is not honest, if this, if the other... Stop putting conditions with the "ifs" and act.

Faith. Jump over the barriers, don't turn them into excuses. If you don't accept challenges, your life will be of a "boring security", whose base is the fear of the new and of change. It may appear secure and comfortable, but it is an illusory security, that may be broken at any moment and in any way.

Acceptance. Mistakes, failures, upsets, disappointments, are part of growth and of knowing the process, and they should not be condemned or feared. Each human being has passed or is passing through them, and it will continue to happen.

Remain light. Everything has its meaning and significance. If not today, in the end you will understand that meaning. It is healthy both for the mind and the body not to weigh oneself down with exaggeration and a lack of perspective.

Life is a game. Know the rules and play it well. A good player is aware, easy, tolerant and flexible, does not stay trapped into a scene, a norm or another player for much time; they give respect and attention, but continue going forward. A good player plays their role and does not try to play that of others.

Respect for being. Recognize your spiritual reality as a human being, with some good inner resources that you should discover and use. Don't accept false external supports, such as name, fame, position, praise. You are what you are because of what is within you. The point of reference is the eternal and valuable, and it is inside you. So you cannot fear that it will be spoilt.

Silence and positive attitude. Realize the importance of being silent from time to time, to re-examine and renew positivism towards yourself and towards life. If not, the speed and immensity of the negative forces of being, or of others, will make you fear again.

Identify Your Values

Our values motivate us; they determine how we live and the direction that we follow in life. Often we don't identify them or articulate them because they are intangible.

To identify your own values you can begin a reflection with the following questions: What is important for you? What are your values as a person and as a professional? What prevents you from putting them into practice? How can you develop or strengthen them? For what value would you surrender your life?

In the process of identifying your values, a practical way that facilitates their recognition is to review the following: Where do your interests and preferences that are transformed into actions, with the underlying values that motivate them, take you? This latter is a first recognition with which you can understand your own values.

The following step consists of determining their relevance in order to be able to focus them better in the situations of each day. What benefits does a value give you? What does knowing your own values bring to you? Recognizing them gives you the possibility to behave with greater security and confidence and, to the extent that you apply them, you start to share them with greater clarity and determination with other people in the duration of the day. Thus, your proposals, projects and actions are filled with content and generate enthusiasm. The process of innovation and personal adjustment is a dialogue that is good for you and that is full of meaning. [12]

In the process of rediscovering your own values, you need to clean out any trace of dishonesty with yourself, since, over time, some habits are generated where there is not honesty, authenticity or total sincerity. If there is not truth or total sincerity, there will be fear. If you want to transform fears, you will have to be totally honest. "The Lord is happy with a sincere heart". Honesty brings you close to God.

When you act basing yourself on sincerity, on honesty and there is not falseness, hypocrisy or deceit, nothing to hide, that is, you are the same on the inside and the outside, you do not create a false image, and that way you free yourself from fear. If you enter the game of saying half-truths or white lies, then you have to tell many other lies to cover over one lie, and that causes certain fears. Exaggerating is also lying: if there are ten, there are ten, why do you say there are fifty? Exaggerating is a way of not expressing reality as it is, but rather basing yourself on a perception that distorts reality.

During the day we accumulate these lies in which there is a lack of honesty and it is said that the person who lies a little, or the one who tells a great lie, are equally liars; the one who steals a pen or steals 10,000 is still a thief, as much the one as the other.

The one who is honest can dance before thousands of people, because they have nothing to hide, they are transparent, authentic. God has given us the freedom to shine. From sincerity, our energy manifests itself with enthusiasm. The self expresses the joy of living. You have a positive vision and you shine.

If you allow there to be transparency in your life, you have nothing to hide: "This is what I am", "This is what has happened to me", "I have made a mistake, forgive me". Easy! You don't need to justify yourself. The ego always needs to justify and justify itself: because of this, because of that, the other, etc. Free yourself of the ego.

To feel whole in your life you have to act in accordance with your values. Don't try to create or offer an image that means being different on the outside to the inside, or act out of greed, selfishness, attachment to dependence. While you continue to act according to those weaknesses or vices, you will continue to have fears and wholeness will seem like a mere utopia.

Resort to the experiences of success, of wholeness, positive memories recorded on your memory. If you have failed some exams and have passed others, you might think that you are going to fail the next one, because you have already failed before. Basing yourself on your experience of failure, you invoke failure, and that way you never break that cycle. What is more, you justify it and, then, as you already go with that awareness of failure to the exam, you fail and, you say: "You see? I was right". You justify your own failure, because you yourself have created it and you have invoked it.

You can do the same with success. The success not of having more, but the success of being better and of being at peace, being happy, having wellbeing, being collaborative and loving; that is, be and express the values. If what you sow is positive, you will reap the positive. You should be aware that you have for a long time been sowing seeds that were mixed with negativity, fears, phobias, useless thoughts, actions based on greed, on selfishness. You need a time to sow and act by centring on positive things and on values, to be able to reach a point of reaping that positivism. It is what is called the law of karma. Each one receives according to what they invoke, according to what they have done and planted in their life.

You can work with visualization and the understanding that you create the future with the present. If in the present you act in response to your values, that is, if your behavior is not motivated by selfishness, greed, anxiety and fear but rather by love, gratitude, cooperation and solidarity, then you are not afraid of the result because you are acting out of good, for the good.

If you respond to good and you heal your life – food, thought, feeling, habits and relationships – you bring health, not only physical but also mental and emotional, into your life. You will be better and you will free yourself of fear. That generates a positive energy that attracts the positive towards you. Positive energy comes into your life.

Perhaps you have lost a friend, but with that positive attitude you create more friends. Perhaps you have had to leave your company and start again, but the learning and growth is better and greater. The saying goes "something good can come out of everything". When you live with that positive attitude and with trust, you feel self-esteem and inner security. The fact of realizing is a great advance. While you are sleeping, you don't see what is happening, and, however, if you realize, it is as if you awoke. In that realizing lies the possibility of change: of a change of attitude, awareness and of motivation in action. You no longer act out of the bitterness brought about by pain, but rather by basing yourself on the values that are at the heart of your being.

You go from being a beggar who begs, needs and desires, to being a giver who gives, donates and collaborates. When you act motivated by love, you transmit a healing energy, because love heals. In the present-day, in each human heart there is a little pain, grief or sadness. Love is a healing energy and necessary revitalizer.

When you act out of those fore-mentioned weaknesses, you ask for protection with fear, you ask to have more with greed, with selfishness you ask for attention, you ask for power. You are in the consciousness of the "I need", "I want". On the contrary, when you act in accordance with your values, as you fill yourself spiritually, from that wholeness you offer love, peace, tranquillity, serenity, happiness and joy. You go from being the one who demands to being the one who offers and gives.

When you mix weaknesses with values, those do not work in the way I am describing. You believe in a value, but you have a habit formed out of greed, and in the action the motivation driven by the value is mixed with the habit formed out of greed. That way you do not receive the results that you could receive and neither does your action have the positive impact that it could have. You have to clean these alloys so that the values work with all their potential in your life.

There are values that are a support and give us the inner power necessary to live the other values in day to day reality. For example, courage, trust and tolerance. Patience is necessary in the process of your awakening and inner change.

I am going to write about these three values. On understanding them and living them, they help you to express the beauty and meaning of values in your life.

COURAGE

Cultivate courage and your heart will be able to open. You are afraid because you want to protect your heart: you feel that something is going to wound it and that is why you hide it, thinking that you are protecting it. You hide it so as not to face being rejected, to not experience failure.

Cultivating courage you awaken your heart, in a way that you no longer need to cover up the most vulnerable part of your being. At the heart of your being there resides the warm tenderness that you have wanted to protect with defences out of fear of being hurt or rejected. By doing that you imprison your heart and do not resolve your inner conflicts nor do you let go of confusion and pain. As you try to cover over this tender part, you generate negativity and resentment in order to "shield" your heart and not let the softest and most tender part be harmed.

With meditation you see clearly all the shields that you have covered yourself with and you begin to let go of that prison that you yourself have created. Open yourself to your feelings, to expressing them and letting go of them, without the need to judge them or justify them.

Cultivate a brave, awake and transparent heart; one that does not need to hide anything. Thus will you develop the skill to mature and be able to live and feel the quality of life without fear. Remember that nobody can hurt you if you do not allow it. If you need to reinforce this, re-read the chapter on Suffering.

Why do you not shine each day, from morning to night? What face do you have when you are frustrated and what one when you are enthused? What face do you have when you are afraid and what one when you are brave, strong and positive?

A sign of loving yourself is to give yourself permission to be brave, to shine with all your potential of inner beauty. Focus on loving yourself, being and shining. That way the old habits will die bit by bit and you will strengthen the habit of being brave.

Build up your self-esteem by generating the habit of being brave and daring to be.

Dare to trust, to take on your own freedom and that of others, to be open to the ideas of others, to be creative, to be wrong and to learn: it is the base of a full and well-lived life.

Dare to dream and be capable of materialising what you dream.
Dare to trust in yourself, in others and in the future of humanity.
Dare to co-operate and share.
Dare to live and enjoy.
Dare to lose control of the situation.
Dare to think in a different way.
Dare to lose securities.
Dare to fail.
Dare to change.
Dare to be.
Dare to be free.
Dare to shine.

Courage is strengthened by cultivating curiosity. We can see it in this example.

In 1911, for reasons that no one has even been able to discover, a man appeared naked and alone at the foot of the Mount Lassen mountains, in North California. With the help of two anthropologists from Berkeley, Thomas Waterman and Alfred Kroeber, it was found out that he was the last remaining member of a tribe of Native American Indians known as the Yana. Although he accepted the friendship of the westerners who took him away and gave him a house at the local university, he never shared his real name and let himself be known as "Ishi", which means "man".

He had never lived in what his benefactors called "civilization", and he was continuously presented with things that he had not experienced before. In his first visit to San Francisco, they took Ishi to the train station. When the train approached, he silently distanced himself from his travel companions and stayed behind a post. When they called him to go with them, he went forward and got on the train. On returning to the university, Kroeber asked him about his strange behaviour on the train station.

Ishi told him that, when he was small, all the members of his tribe saw the train pass through the valley. Observing it, they saw how it dragged itself forward giving off smoke that seemed to come from some fire inside the train, and that made them think that it was a devil that ate people. Surprised, Kroeber asked: "How is it that you had the courage to get on the train if you thought it was a devil?"

Ishi responded: "My life has shown me to have more curiosity than fear".

TRUST AND FAITH

Believe in Yourself

Trust in life and that beauty and truth are possible. You have to believe in yourself and your own possibilities, in your own capacity for transformation, in your own capacity for ethical, positive and right action. Believe in your intuition. On believing in yourself, you trust that others are going to help you to achieve your aims that are set out honestly and passionately.

Trust is a basic disposition with which to flow through life and deal with its uncertainties and complexities with a certain degree of emotional success. Without trust there is not hope, freedom, tolerance or the possibility of learning from one's mistakes, which means that building one's self-esteem becomes somewhat difficult.

Get Your Trust Back

Hellenic wisdom denominated the term trust, *empistosini*, or "to believe in", derived from the Latin and that, in fact, should be translated by "without bail", "sin fiducia" or "garment that gives the contractor the security of the correct fulfilment of their oblig-ation".

Without trust, without shared faith, we cannot realize projects together.

We are in a world in which the trust has been lost; there is not trust between business partners, between parents and children, between work colleagues, in the government, between our leaders, whether political or religious. Even in life as a couple trust is broken and there is pain and separation. It is a world where trust has been lost. There is mistrust between countries. There is a lack of trust and there is fear about what is going to happen. Trust has disappeared around us. Violence and aggression abound. How much money is spent on security today, be it security in our homes or at the airports? And my question is: Is there more safety because of this security? Do I sleep more soundly if I have high walls and a security system surrounding me? Is there more security in a nation if there is more security in an airport? I understand the need for all these external aspects. But let us look at the factors that have brought us to all this.

The factors that have brought us to insecurity include the lack of faith in ourselves, the lack of trust in the other near to us and the lack of faith in God. That has generated enormous divisions between different sectors of humanity; racial, cultural, social and even religious divisions. Fear is increasing in society because of this. To be able to resolve this, we can only bring spiritual energy, the sacred and God into our lives.

Our greatest contribution to peace in the world consists of getting back and reestablishing our inner peace. The method is meditation and it begins with a vital but simple truth: "I am a soul and my true nature is peace".

When you know yourself as a spiritual being, a child of God, you trust yourself. In that awareness as a child of God you recognize your intrinsic, eternal goodness.

Each human being has a heart of gold – it is a reality. When you spend time in silence, connected to yourself, you begin to trust in that heart of gold. In the awareness of your spiritual identity you can connect with God. When you have a live relationship with God, you can trust Him because you feel the protection and blessings of God. When you re-establish trust in yourself and trust in God, you can trust in the goodness of the people that surround you. In that state any need to be afraid disappears.

Trust Bonds and Unites

Deep trust generates the creation of solid and stable human bonds and is the main source of commitment and fidelity in the interpersonal relationship. Without true trust there is not free commitment. Trust acts as "cohesive glue" to the relationships between people, groups, organizations and societies. Without trust there is a lack of organisational and social bonding, disintegration, interpersonal fragmentation.

The free decision to trust can be situated in a continuum that goes from deep trust to active mistrust. One thing is the trust or belief in oneself or self-trust; another, trust in others, in the future of humanity, in our political leaders or in the company project in which one might be participating; and another, trust of others towards us, or trustworthiness.

We generate trust when we show ourselves whole, we want the good of the other, we demonstrate a capacity to resolve their needs, we adopt a positive emotional tone and we maintain good self-esteem. Both people and social systems are more disposed towards trust if they have inner security, if they have good self-esteem and trust in themselves, if they are within themselves in an empowered way.

We tend to trust in others and to love them to the extent that we trust in ourselves and have a high self-esteem. It is easier to trust someone who has self-esteem. [13]

Faith in Action

The word "faith" is associated to what is not visible, but is real: the soul. Faith in consciousness, in your inner identity and in your destiny. Faith in the consciousness of the divine. Faith in yourself is connected with that because not only are you aware that you are a soul, but also a child of God. That faith of knowing that you are a child of God changes your awareness completely. Basing yourself on that faith you can trust in others because you see them as children of God. If you see others on a level of external identity, you observe a great difference between some and others. There exists such a great difference that that vision means to feel that there are big walls that separate us.

I am using the word "faith" and I want to connect it with "trust". Faith lives within your inner consciousness and in your understanding. Trust is expressed in relationships. Where you do not have faith, it is not possible to trust. Begin by having faith in yourself, knowing who you are; faith in your spiritual identity. Faith is not associated with your outward appearance or identity of gender, race, build, physical appearance. In none of those aspects is it a question of faith.

Empistosini means "to have faith or believe in". To be convinced, to have faith, believe in oneself, in others or in some ideal, is the base from which to dare to live and allow others to live with credibility, security and joy.

In the faith that I am a soul, in the faith that I am a child of God, I trust in the fact that you are also that spiritual being, a child of God. And in that trust that you are a divine being, I am capable of recognizing the goodness that there is in you, so our relationship is based on the awareness of our eternal divinity, and, thus, the relationship changes in an extraordinary way. I am no longer afraid of you, but rather I can trust in you. The fear of the other disappears, even the one that you do not know. You are aware that the other is also a being created by God, a child of God. You respect them because of this.

In situations of risk or insecurity, you will have seen that you have to take the step of courage that means putting your faith and trust in action over and above logic. In those moments, logical reasoning tells you that it cannot be done or that it is not possible. But the faith and trust that motivate you at that moment make you not think out of logic. At that moment, you do what you have to do out of the faith that moves you.

On the 12th September 2001 I received an email from a friend, Ram Prakash, teacher of meditation of the Brahma Kumaris centre in New York. He told me his experience of the previous day. Ima Sanchís decided to interview him for "La Contra". What follows is the example that this New Yorker of Indian origin gave us. In a situation of extreme insecurity and confusion, his faith and trust helped him to save himself and to save other lives. This is his testimony: [14]

"I am a structural engineer and I work for the World Trade Centre as a manager of infrastructure. I have been collaborating with the Brahma Kumaris University for seventeen years. I believe in universal peace and I do not believe in revenge. When the terrorist attack took place I was there, in the North Tower, the first to receive the impact and the last to collapse. I work on the 64th floor.

When the explosion happened, at quarter to nine in the morning, there were 150 work colleagues in the office. The building began to tremble. The glass panes broke and the metal from the walls fell on us.

I reacted quite calmly. We had done evacuation drills in case of accident and we knew what we had to do, so we went down the stairs in an orderly manner.

We went down thirty floors through a thick smoke that hardly let us breathe. We went in file, very close together. At that height of the building the people were crowded together on the staircase and we couldn't continue to descend. We let the burnt people go past first and some of them we had to carry on our backs.

I guided my group. I have been doing meditation for seventeen years. The breathing exercises were very useful to me in controlling the feeling of suffocation. The meditation helped me to be more relaxed and to deal with the events more calmly. This made the others follow me.

On the 33rd floor, the situation got more complicated. We had to wait for a long time in the middle of the smoke. There was complete confusion. While we were trying to continue going down, a group of firemen were going up. Seeing how they were risking their lives for us gave us encouragement. Afterwards, most of those men were trapped. That is hard to deal with, but I hold tight to the idea that good exists.

"When the South Tower fell we had reached floor 20 and we heard another big explosion. All the building felt the shaking and it threw us to the ground. At that moment we knew that something horrendous was happening. Our exit was becoming slower and more desperate, the smoke was unbreathable, people were shouting and crying. I managed to keep calm.

When we were already nearing the ground floor, the water pipes exploded. A cascade of water formed which went down the stairs with great force. People were slipping and hurting themselves. The panic was growing. We were in the dark, and walking with the water covering our feet and over 25 centimetres of rubble through a corridor that was completely dark and full of smoke. All the wires were hanging over our heads.

When we reached the outside, there was fire everywhere and the heat created a great movement of rubble; it was very difficult to move forward. When we managed to get out of the devastated area there was a new thunderous noise and all the ground trembled. We all ran holding on to each other to get away. The tower was collapsing and we had just come out of it. At that moment, with a group of people, we went to the meditation centre on Fifth Avenue, next to 33rd Street. I was terribly affected, but happy with myself because I was capable of helping others and did not think only of saving myself. I think I owe all that to meditation; I was capable of uniting mind and soul. I believe deeply in peace.

I told my companions to be brave; I encouraged them to keep faith and trust. I myself am surprised at having been able to breathe almost normally and having been able to guide people through the smoke and rubble. I felt apart from that catastrophe, as if I was off the stage. I felt like a child watching a play. I think it is the moment to look within and find God inside me.

In 1993 I was also the victim of another terrorist attempt at the World Trade Centre. On that occasion I escaped 10 minutes before.

I believe in destiny; for me, God is destiny and the supreme justice."

The above experience is a clear example of faith in action.

Trust Awakens Goodness

I would like to share a story about how trust awakens goodness in the human being. In many countries, particularly in England, the teachers of the Brahma Kumaris University carry out services and activities in the prisons. We work with the prison personnel and we hold retreats for them, but we also work with the prisoners. We participate in programmes that are included in the Department of Education for prisons. We talk to them about positive thinking, about meditation, self-esteem and that improves the atmosphere that there is in the group.

A few years ago, a prisoner had studied meditation with the teacher that used to go to the prison to teach him. One of their activities had been in the carpentry department and he made a very pretty table and chair for Dadi, the international director of the Brahma Kumaris World Spiritual University. He wanted to organise an event at the prison, a kind of ceremony in which he could give Dadi that gift: a table and a chair.

The Director of the Department of Education of that prison was a person who understood the importance of doing things with respect and dignity and decided that yes, they would do it, and that they would have a special ceremony. Some 50 men got together for that ceremony. It had been announced that the invitation was open to whoever wanted to go and, basically, they were men who had been participating in the courses that we had given there. The director of the Department of Education, when receiving us, told us: "These men have prepared the ceremony and the program themselves; I didn't say anything to them - they have planned it themselves".

What they decided to do was to meet Dadi and look at her in the eyes, because, when we meditate, we do so with our eyes open and some of them knew this. They wanted to have the experience of being close to her and maintain an exchange of looks while each one gave her a flower. One by one, they gave Dadi a flower and had that exchange of looks. Thanks to this a powerful and beautiful atmosphere was created. Dadi spoke to them about spiritual aspects, about values and about meditation. They presented her with the table and chair in an atmosphere generated by a feeling of trust.

The prison education director asked Dadi: "Dadi, do you know why these men are here in the prison?" Each one of the men in that group had killed someone, including the person who had made the table. I do not know the story of each of those people, but in that situation with Dadi what happened is that something good had awoken inside them.

In people, independently of what they may have done in their lives, there is something of goodness and divinity in each human heart. If we see people with that trust, we awaken that goodness in them. There are atmospheres that bring about violence. You can choose to be the creator of atmospheres that make the goodness of others emerge.

I have told of the experience of an extreme example with people who are shut away in prisons. However, you can apply this principle so that trust awakens goodness in your own family. Independently of whether you have children or not, we have all been children, we remember those experiences. When you trust in your son and in your daughter, that son and daughter will respond to that trust.

If you do not trust in your child, that child will respond to your lack of trust. Trust in your business partners, secretaries, collaborators, students. Trust in people and the good will emerge. That is the experience of many. Trust is not something that is simply comfortable. If you are surrounded by an atmosphere of mistrust, you will feel very uncomfortable, but when you are in an atmosphere of trust, it will be natural, comfortable and easy.

Trust awakens the highest potential in the human being.

Agility and Creativity

When you trust in yourself you dare to be creative and to respond with agility in the face of situations, people and events. When you trust, you are open to dialogue, to maintaining the relationship, to mutual support and learning, to creative initiative.

You are a source of inspiration that, with your presence, allow others to let go and be creative.

On one occasion, Jagdish Chander, a Raj Yogi teacher from India, who died a few years ago, told us that he had gone to New York. There they told him that, although the shortest way to get to a certain place was on a specific street, it was dangerous to go down it, and it was better to go round another way. But he thought he could go the shorter way. He was halfway along the street when four men appeared, threatening him.

He asked them if they knew the typical dance from India and started to dance. Then, those men smiled, that is, they changed from having a threatening face to a smiling one. The innocence of this response must have reached them and they let him go and Jagdish went dancing down the street. That kind of response can only come from a person who is sure of themselves, who is not afraid and does not have their creativity blocked. Another would start shouting, trembling, would be paralysed, would faint, would throw themselves to the ground, in sum, they would have a response of trauma and panic.

The human being has the capacity to respond with creativity, with love, positivism, as long as he/she has a good level of self-esteem, of personal security, of trust, clarity and is not afraid. Because of this they have the power to confront. They also have the capacity to observe from a distance. It is what in other words we could define as being a detached observer, that is, that you observe the situation, the scene, without implicating yourself. You do not attach yourself to it; you do not get caught in it. You keep a certain distance, as if it were a film. Therefore, you do not let yourself be influenced by it and you can control yourself and control it.

You maintain your serenity, you accept and face the situation, understanding its meaning and freeing yourself of its impact. Thus you have a creative response to resolve that problem and you do not allow it to take away your inner wellbeing.

You can practice an exercise of observation in silence: relax. Breathe deeply. Think: I am not this situation. I separate myself from it. I tranquillize my mind. I think: nothing is permanent. Everything will pass.

You need to have that capacity to free yourself of the influences that diminish you, those that deaden you; those that reduce your capacity to love, to shine, to feel yourself as free, to be at peace. Those influences come from outside and also from your past and your habits.

You need silence, patience, the capacity of reflection in order not to react immediately responding out of fear and insecurity, but rather responding from values, trust, respect, listening, tolerance, creativity and inner strength.

You need to clean out the cupboards of your mind, the archives that are in your soul so that no habit leads you to react with bitterness, jealousy, hate, fear.

To reach that state of wholeness where there is a balance between mind and heart, you need to feel by responding to your values, overcoming the feelings that are blocking that experience, strengthen your self-esteem, clarity, self-control and personal governance and develop the powers that will help you to face problems and overcome influences.

TOLERANCE

It is important to understand that to overcome problems you need, on the one hand, inner power, and, on the other, the capacity to tolerate. Tolerating does not mean to put up with. To tolerate is to accept, understand and know how to face things. That is, to tolerate is not to put up with and then explode. In tolerance you dissolve that which, otherwise you would be putting up with. It is like the sea, which is an example of tolerance, because we throw a lot of dirt into the sea, the sea absorbs it and, over time, transforms it. Tolerance is being like the ocean, that is, knowing how to absorb and dissolve, make disappear.

Tolerance has to be balanced with the capacity to face things, which is based on bravery, courage and personal security. Having the power to tolerate gives you security and trust that you will be able to, you will achieve it, and you will advance. Tolerance is necessary for shared living, to be and allow to be. With the virtue of tolerance, you will continue to smile, you will never be discouraged. To smile when someone praises you is not to be tolerant. However, when someone turns into an angry enemy and insults you, but you do not have even the slightest sign of dejection on your face, not even in your thoughts, that is to be tolerant. To look, to speak and to enter in contact with feelings of compassion, patience, comprehension, love and respect, with a person that you do not have a good relationship with, is to have tolerance.

In the ancient sacred texts of India, Mahavir Hanuman has been portrayed as carrying a great mountain in his hand as if it were a ball. It does not matter if the problem, obstacle or storm seems like a great mountain: turn something that appears as big as a mountain into a small toy, and overcome it as if it were a game. Make something big be very light, and you yourself will feel light. Don't turn a small stone into a mountain; turn the mountain into a ball. To take the expansion to its essence is tolerance.

Expanding obstacles and problems in your mind or speaking of them to others means to create mountains. Don't go into expansion: put a full stop and turn over the page and that way you will advance.

A tolerant person is always capable of taking expansion, problems and obstacles to their essence with knowledge, meditation and silence. When you choose the longest road, doing so consumes more and ends up by exhausting your time and energy. Expansion is the longest road and the essence is to take a shortcut. Both work in order to get to the other side, but thanks to those who take a shortcut being able to save their time and energy, they do not get discouraged. They constantly enjoy themselves and overcome everything with a smile. That is being tolerant.

Someone who has the power of tolerance will never be afraid or think: "Why is this happening to me too?" As they are constantly full, they will go deeper into the knowledge and the memory of what is essential in life. The one who is afraid is not capable of going deeper. That's why there is depth in something that is full (wholeness). The one who has expansion is empty; for this reason, something that is empty resounds and the person devotes themselves to prattling away. The one who has wholeness is silent; the one who is empty speaks a lot and does not say anything.

Someone who lives in expansion will be constantly murmuring saying things like: "Why this? What is this? This should not be like that but rather in this way. It shouldn't be like that". This person will continue talking in this way in their thoughts and in their words, and also in front of everybody. What happens when you chatter away, beyond the limits? Your murmuring leaves you dry, out of breath and you tire. Those who are tolerant are saved from all these things and for this reason they always feel enjoyment and bliss, they do not chatter but rather fly in the wholeness of their inner silence.

When you have developed the power of tolerance, you do things with pleasure. Whether it is a routine physical job or whether you have to give a talk on a stage in front of hundreds of people, you do both things with pleasure. This is living a life of pleasure. I am not referring to the physical pleasures but rather to living a life with pleasure in your heart, and that way you will be able to transform any situation or task from confusion into pleasure.

Life teaches you that you can widen the limits of your tolerance. When certain situations arrive, they are like exams in order to see your capacity to tolerate. These exams can first be the unpleasant words and harassment by people towards you. Secondly, the different obstacles that place themselves in your path, making it difficult to carry out your aims. There are also people that you trust who will oppose you. Your work colleagues or your partners turn into your enemies and create opposition because they are not happy about small or big matters.

With the feeling of satisfying those who are not happy, considering that they are influenced by something, holding on to benevolent feelings and with the power of silence and tolerance, you can make others advance, overcome and collaborate. You can teach the lesson of tolerance with sweetness, good desires and pure feelings. That way not only do you advance, but you are also a light on the road so that others can also advance.

Learn to tolerate with wellbeing. Stabilise yourself in your inner being and, from that calm, clarity and stability you can tolerate without losing your wellbeing. To tolerate is to accept, value, understand and appreciate. Not making a mountain out of a molehill but rather the contrary, by taking expansion to the essence.

WHOLENESS

Reaching wholeness is one of the most sought after objectives of the human being. The question is what is understood by wholeness, what it is to be whole, and how that state is reached.

From East to West, from South to North, there exists a great diversity of concepts about wholeness and proposals about how to reach it: from the most spiritual wholeness to the intellectual, from the emotional to the materialist, from the battle for power to the effort to acquire and have more and more. At bottom, what we want is to fill the inner emptiness that sometimes invades us, and to feel ourselves full and useful, and to shine with all our strengths. In that sense, wholeness is not a "final" state but rather we can feel it in the here and now. It is a matter of accepting and feeling that you are in the place you have to be in, at the moment that you have to be, doing what you have to do. That is, the total acceptance of your situation. And if you do not accept it, you can change the situation or change situation. To achieve it, you need to dare to generate the necessary change to feel fine, to know how to let go of what ties you to the situation and to resolve what generates conflict and dissatisfaction in you.

The uneasy and unpeaceful mind asks itself: "Why is this happening to me?" "I would like to be in another place at this moment". "I would like to do something else now". "If this person changes, I will feel better". With an endless list of desires that appear in the mind, generating dissatisfactions, comparing yourself to another, wanting what the other has, complaining and wanting the other to change, you stop appreciating who you are, what you have and who you are with. That dissatisfaction produced by a mind that jumps from one desire to another like a wild and uncontrolled horse distances you from the wholeness that you could feel right now.

To enjoy the present moment, to savour it, means to have your mind under control, to be concentrated and focused on what you are doing right now. To be yourself. At the end of the day, the only thing you really have is you, your mind and the present moment.

Anything can happen in the next instant, but worrying about what might happen, lamenting what already happened or complaining about what is happening now; the wholeness of that moment will escape you. Out of stress, pressure or confusion, the mind thinks a lot but does not reach the creative solutions that allow you to feel whole in your decisions and in your actions, and in the evaluation of their repercussions in your life.

When something happens that you were not expecting, embracing the unforeseen and accepting the change helps you to carry on shining in the wholeness of that instant. That means to tolerate the unforeseen, change, the situation or people. To tolerate understood not as uselessly putting up with but rather as acceptance and full understanding, from which there is openness to dialogue and to change. The combination of tolerance with the capacity to face things arises out of bravery and personal security. This gives you the trust and conviction that you will be able to achieve it, that you will go forward and reach your objective.

You need a tranquil mind, which in silence can find the creative solutions to tolerate, face things and change. Out of silence, the mind creates with wholeness.

You need silence, patience, the capacity for reflection in order not to react in an immediate way out of fear and insecurity, but rather to respond out of the values, love, respect, listening, tolerance, creativity and inner strength. It is about responses that arise from the wholeness of your being. They are non-violent responses that generate harmony around you. To quieten the mind you have to evoke the inner power of your being, that is, your values and your innate strength, the power to discern with clarity and your capacity for decision free of negative influences – inner ones such as fear, or outer ones such as certain opinions of others.

Making decisions under the influence of fear will never lead you to the wholeness of your being or the clarity of your ideas. To strengthen yourself, you have to free yourself from some weaknesses and complexes; stop comparing yourself to others; accept yourself and strengthen your qualities to be yourself.

Free yourself from the influences that deaden you, from those that diminish your capacity to love, to shine, to feel yourself free, to be at peace. Those influences come from the outside and they also arise from within you, that is, they are based on the recordings of your past and your habits, your beliefs, your way of thinking and your limited perception of reality.

You will come to enjoy a serene mind when you are at peace with your past and accept the present, when your life is coherent and integral, when your conscience is peaceful and you are capable of controlling the flow of your thoughts. Then, you will be capable of transforming the creation of useless, superfluous and negative thoughts to begin to create thoughts full of beauty and harmony, making your mind finally become your ally in reaching the wholeness of your being.

Wholeness is that state in which there is a harmony in your being: spiritual, mental, emotional and physical; there is coherence between thought, word and action. Your creativity is not blocked and there is serenity in your soul. Your feelings and actions are based on values such as love, peace and happiness, you are satisfied and you feel freed.

Fear, insecurity, attachment and dependence block your experience of love, peace, serenity, freedom and happiness. You should face and overcome those energies so that there is more harmony and wholeness in your life.

Cultivate your values, nourish your soul and strengthen yourself to overcome those blockages, and that way you will reach a state of wholeness in which your life has meaning, you love your life and what you do.

Strengthen yourself by knowing yourself, learning to govern your inner energies. Understand where what you think, what you feel, comes from and where what you are thinking takes you. Strengthen your self-esteem, your capacity to respect yourself and love yourself. When you improve your self-esteem, you strengthen your capacity to overcome fears and you get back your inner power.

In order to live in the present in the maximum wholeness of being, it is necessary:

- To be conscious, to be "awake" and to take responsibility for how you are and what you feel and do.
- To be inwardly strong: get back your inner power.
- To listen to your intuition and your heart.
- To live and appreciate in the present, heal the burdens that you carry from your past, visualize a better future, with a clear aim of achieving it.
- To let go of your past.
- To change harmful and unhealthy habits.
- To create healthy habits.
- To live the values.
- To ask yourself positive questions.
- To believe in yourself, love yourself, dare to be yourself with all its consequences.
- To trust and have faith.
- To get back your spirituality. Incorporate sacred and divine energy into your daily life.
- To enjoy out of the silence.
- To maintain hope.
- To meditate in order to achieve all these objectives!

AWAKENING

Even when we are awake and conscious of the world that surrounds us, it is as if we were asleep and incapable of seeing the world as it is, incapable of seeing others as they really are and incapable of seeing events in their true light. We see, we perceive and we interpret reality.

Our intellect perceives the world and interprets it according to past beliefs and experiences. If we learn to believe that we are bodies and not souls, that our emotions are created by others, and that the world evolves in a positive and progressive way, those beliefs will influence our vision, perception and interpretation of the behaviour of other people, situations and world events in a certain way. Our thoughts, emotions and conduct respond to that. Each one of these three beliefs is wrong. Check it for yourself.

In essence, we have our eyes closed in the face of truth; that is why we go through life asleep and don't even know it. Due to erroneous convictions, we will create some form of suffering or pain on some intimate level, but we will put up with that pain believing that it must be something normal. Only when the suffering becomes very intense do we recognize that we have to do something. And here we are, doing something about it, reading this book to see if it helps us to understand the pain and fear and helps us to transform it or overcome it. The mere fact of reading the book is not sufficient to reach a real and lasting transformation; only the practice of meditation and in-depth study of the truths about the identity of being will heal our emotional, mental and spiritual pain.

The meditation and spiritual analysis that we are developing will help us to awaken and to remain with our eyes open in the face of the deepest realities of life that surround us and in the face of the eternal truths that are already to be found in us.

We all have the capacity to observe instead of sleep, to awaken to the reality of spirit (of which we are) and offer our envigorating power to those who remain asleep around us. When someone awakens spiritually, their intuition awakens, the voice of their soul, the voice that says that in reality it wants to free itself of fears and ties. That voice is normally deadened by an intellect that is constantly analyzing, criticising, blaming and judging. It remains deadened by a mind that is dispersed and controlled by fear.

On awakening the spirit, we banish the fear that our relationships with others cause us and give room to love in its place. In reality, nobody can hurt us. On extending our forgiveness to those who treat us with little consideration, we accumulate the spiritual merit of generating a good karma and we receive blessings. The blessings emanate from an awakened heart and awaken those who receive them.

Anthony de Mello speaks of awakening: "If you manage to keep your spirit free of obstacles and your senses open, you will begin to perceive things as they are and to establish a mutual interaction with reality, and you will be captured by the harmony of the universe. Then you will understand what God is, because you will have finally understood what love is". [15]

There are habits, seductively pleasurable attachments, that prevent us from reaching our potential. We live dominated by those habits that keep us in a state of somnolence. We have to wake up. As people we should become conscious of our capacity to live with greater wholeness. We live in a state of ignorance, of lethargy.

To awaken, that is, to see things with clarity. To be aware of the impact that your thoughts, your beliefs and your vision have on your life and your relationships. To see that you, now, can be happy. Whilst you don't believe it, you don't achieve it, and whilst you don't see it, you don't come to experience it or live it, an awakening that means to be responsible and be conscious of the need to co-operate, show solidarity and live in the values, have a wide and global vision that includes the spiritual dimension.

In reality, in origin, we are free. We only have to push gently at the door of our cell (created by our limited perception of reality) to open it little by little and be capable of walking in the pure light of being. The faculty that advises us of this freedom is intuition, often called the sixth sense.

Intuition and Forms of Intuitive or Intellectual Perception

In life there are many situations for which nobody gives you instructions; it is your own intuition and your decision in that moment that saves you from an accident or that protects you from a negative influence, and vice versa. There is a growing understanding that neither the intellectual mode nor the intuitive in isolation can give us a complete vision of reality.

Meditation helps you to awaken that intuition and differentiate it from your ego. Different voices speak to you: the voice of your ego, the one influenced by your past, by the people you depend on or have attachments to, the voice of other people's opinions, that of your desires; that of your logic and the voice of your intuition connected to your consciousness. Sometimes they all speak to you: Which one do you listen to? How do you decide? Meditation will help you to clarify that inner world of voices and you listen to the voice of innate wisdom. Psychologists have distinguished two different forms of perception: the intuitive and the intellectual. They have reached the conclusion that contemporary science favours the intellectual mode of awareness and that the old spiritual traditions favour the intuitive mode. Intuitive perception is applied there where the dimension goes beyond the five senses. Without the dimension of knowledge and experience, intuitive perception can investigate into the region of fantasy.

In present-day civilisation based on materialism, more importance is given to the mode of intellectual perception and generally we tend to deny the development of the intuitive mode. However, the life style in older societies, such as the adiwasis in the remote mountains of India, the kooris of Australia or the Native Americans, has a different basis. The people who follow these ancient practices are in tune with nature and, sometimes, even with supernatural phenomenon. In these surroundings, the intuitive mode is considered to be a very important life skill.

These differences of perception have generated a lot of controversy and debates about the nature of the universe in the scientific community. However, there is an increasing recognition and appreciation that our vision of reality is determined by our consciousness. There are more and more researchers who have tried to synthesise the two visions and find points in common. *The Tao of Physics*, by Fritjof Capra; *Mysticism and New Physics*, by Michael Talbot; *Dancing Wu Li Masters*, by Gary Zukov; and *Supernature*, by Lyall Watson. This has led us to more in-depth studies of the old mystical and spiritual traditions. Many sociologists, psychologists, anthropologists, psychiatrists and even some physicists have tried to understand the theoretical aspects and practices of Buddhism, Christianity, Hinduism, Sufism and other traditions. These are some of the well-known books, published in the West in the 70s and 80s, that juxtapose science and spirituality.

The perception of beauty, the value and the sacred of life is the mystical and spiritual basis of all religions and the reference point from which to form teachings of the moral and the values. The scientific vision of the world gives importance to sensorial data, to rational thinking and to material values such as money, property and social status, etc., due to an inability to perceive or demonstrate the human spirit.

I would like to clarify the use of the word "intuition". Just as with other words like "love" or "peace", we use the term "intuition" to describe sensations that are far from what the word really means. For example, it is often used to designate any premonition, any altered state of consciousness, any instinctive reaction; any forecast of a matter that (even when the solution is correct) would not have more than a mediocre reach or interest. In this meaning, the (supposed) intuition would be something very different to the concept that I am referring to, which is the base of intuitive perception that the oldest spiritual traditions speak of to us and for sure have little or nothing to do with the reality of the state in which pure intuition is awake. On the contrary, uncountable bad things have come about from those supposed intuitions. Other times it is alleged that one has "an intuition" when a question presents itself as difficult, heavy or slow to resolve correctly and lucidly, and one takes an impulsive option or on the base of only a partial appreciation. Also in this case it is about something very different to the meaning of "intuition" that we are setting out from and that I have explained previously.

A sure intuition and one that manifests itself with at least relative frequency implies and supposes a solid intellectual and spiritual development, as well as maturity and emotional intelligence. Even more: although the great advances in the field of knowledge and creativity are invariably due to intuitions, these do not happen in a void or without a cause that propitiates them; only in the previously worked mental terrain (which has become simultaneously awake and receptive) through a vigorous and sustained effort of "more light". Only after the effort of an intense wanting and devoted to the good of a global, precise and unselfish solution, can this solemn "religious" experience take place, which does not mean that intuition is limited to acting in matters belonging to the area of religions. Intuition can project light onto any area of knowledge and creativity. The coinciding testimonies of so many geniuses in the history of humanity show that it is thus.

In western terminology, "intuition" is a way of expressing that unifying wisdom, full of exactitude, of life, creativity and love. Intuition is the word that allows us access to an intimate, real and essential wisdom, which comes from direct contact with the essence, with reality, with the intimate nature of beings and phenomenon. Intuition represents the source of true discernment between good and bad, between truth and falsity, between right and wrong, and the possibility of a real and transtemporal wisdom (different from a knowledge that is superficial and based on the always mutable sensorial illusion). Such intuition supposes a previous and diligent complete personal development, at least so that it can become trustworthy and relatively frequent. The meditation and study that awakens spiritual intelligence favours that exact clarity, that certain and shining knowledge, that penetration into the essential reality of the universe, that luminous spiritual consciousness, that unifying comprehension that includes one's own intuition.

Intuition is the line of union between the personal and the universal, the diverse and the one, material and spirit; it is the understanding of what beauty is, what certainty is, and what creativity is; what power is and what serenity is; what is permanence and what is discovery. Intuition is the strength of the pioneer, the inspiration of the genius, the brilliance of the creator, both in art and in science, in religion as in philosophy, in politics as in any other field where the effort of knowledge, of progress, of creativity, of the perfectioning and of service to the general good can take place. An enormous list of the greatest figures of the history of humanity left it deliberately expressed that intuition was the inspiring light that opened the way to them for their most important works.

So we can understand that true intuition constitutes something relatively rare in humanity, and it is regrettable that the reference to that lived perception is vulgarised when it only causes premonitions, foreboding, instincts, and "very strong sensations".

To become truly intuitive is the result of a long and persistent evolutionary effort that presupposes a great previous personal, spiritual, mental, intellectual and emotional development, not only on their concrete levels but also on the most subtle ones.

Gottfried Purucker says that: "intuition is the organ of direct knowledge; it is the clothing of the divine spark in us, which not only instantaneously recognizes the truth, but also communicates it, if the barriers are not too dense and heavy between it and our receptive minds". Our individual Buddhi (our spiritual intelligence) is what gives us intuition, discernment, the sensitivity to respond rapidly to the suffering and pain of others". [16]

The Mirror to See Yourself In
We have seen that intuition is the faculty of an awakened consciousness: it allows you to realize, to have a vision that is

global and connected to spiritual intelligence. On awakening, you realize the urgent necessity of bringing about certain changes in your life. To overcome and transform the fears of change, which emerge when you begin to realize and to "awaken", it is important to know yourself and understand yourself. To know yourself you need silence, introspection, time, discipline, observation, knowledge and meditation. You only have to set yourself to it. While you are judging and criticizing others, you are seeing the other, not yourself. Physically you do not see your face, unless it is with a mirror. Others see your face, but not you. You need a mirror. To see yourself spiritually and realize what you are like within, you need a mirror.

On a mental, emotional and spiritual level, what is the mirror that helps you to see yourself to realize what is happening to you and what you have to do? Where do you have to cleanse? Where do you have to scrape? What do you have to do? What is happening in your mind, in your heart, in your soul and in your being? Why do you get depressed over and over again? Why do you have fears? Why do you have phobias? Why do you get irritated? What are the causes and roots of your grief or suffering?

Look for the answers inside you. There will always be external influences, but you shouldn't allow the river into your boat to sink you. The river is life and you are the boat. When you allow the situations of life to get into you, you sink. You can respond to external influences without sinking into them.

Your soul wants to be free. So, why do you tie yourself down? It wants to love. So, why do you attach yourself? It wants to be strong. So, why do you weaken yourself? You do not listen to your inner voice and you do not allow your pure intuition to openly manifest itself. From the awakening and the application of spiritual intelligence in your life you connect to your true purpose, with what you want and where you want to go.

The mirror to see yourself in, to be connected to your true purpose, is given to you by the knowledge of wisdom and the eternal spiritual truths. In the silence of meditation you open yourself to the wisdom of your being. Thus do you connect with your inner awareness, with the depth of your being, with what your soul really wants.

Each day you need to listen to or read a piece of knowledge that broadens the horizons of your limited vision, that connects you to the essence of your being and keeps your spiritual intelligence awake. Socrates already told us: "Only the knowledge that makes us better is useful to us".

On meditating, you visualize and you feel your true being, luminous and free of all influences, That experience helps you to see yourself as you really are and in contrast to how you are now. Perhaps you *feel* bad, weak, feeble, but in reality you *are* strong. Meditation offers you the mirror to see the contrast between feeling and being and to iron out the differences.

What you think is invisible to others and only you know what it is. But you transmit your thoughts through your expressions, your words and in your actions on relating to others and to the world. That way your words and your actions act as a mirror in which to see yourself. You achieve this when you are an observer and you become aware of your responses, your reactions and how you express what arises from within you.

When you talk a lot you repeat things, you justify yourself and you say a lot of useless things, which is a sign that you think too much. Realize this and start to think less; that way your words will be more forceful and will carry a clearer message. Talking less, talking with sweetness, talking with respect, is the sign of an awake, serene, careful and attentive mind. As Euripedes said: "Talk if you have more important words than the silence, if not keep quiet".

Your Attitude in the Face of Change

Change according to the spiritual point of view is the essence of the material world: everything changes and there is change at all moments, we cannot prevent it.

Life is change; at each moment there are changes; the Earth is

constantly turning, nothing is still, nothing is permanent, everything changes. When we like something, we want it to stay like
that. We have to learn to like it in its change. You know a person,
you like them as they are, you like them like that, and you want
them to be like that always. But that person changes and you do
too. Adapting to change is very important in order not to get
frustrated and to continue enjoying yourself in each instant.

We have created our own inner cages where we feel more or
less comfortable. We fear leaving that box, that label, that identity
that is known to us and feeds our fear of changing, our fear of the
different, of the unknown.

The psychotherapist and neurologist Viktor Frankl who was a
Jewish survivor of the Nazi concentration camps, reminds us:
"Man can be stripped of everything, except one thing: the last of
the human freedoms, the freedom to choose the attitude that one
adopts in the face of any set of circumstances and of choosing one's
own destiny". [17]

You have the freedom and the capacity to choose how to
respond in the face of situations: to accept, deal with and change,
or to resist, fear, reject and flee. What you resist persists and what
you accept is transformed. The inflexibility that arises out of fear
and resistance blocks you and is the catalyst of the destruction of
one's own capacity to live fully, without blockages.

If you do not face a situation, you flee from it with fear. There is
another option: you can stay serene and deal with the situation,
understanding its significance and freeing yourself from its impact.
Flow with it without succumbing to it.

On other occasions it is not that you are afraid of change but
rather that you change out of fear of... Don't base your decisions
and changes on the fear of conflict, of not being understood, of
losing someone or something, of being rejected, of not being liked,
of ending up alone. The changes that are based on fear are usually
not very solid and do not always give good results. Don't consider
an obstacle as such or the person who has been the instrument that
created the obstacle as a person who brings obstacles, but rather

see them as your teacher in order to become an experienced being and to strengthen you. The one who slanders you is your friend, the one who makes you face your own obstacles, and makes you thus have experience, maturity and increases your capacity to face and tolerate; they are your teacher.

A Hindu proverb says thus: "No man is your enemy; all men are your teachers".

Keep an open attitude to learning and you will live through changes better.

Perhaps you find yourself with a situation that you see in the shape of an obstacle, or a person places obstacles before you. You can change your way of seeing it, given that, in fact, they become an instrument in helping you to overcome obstacles, to become strong and to make you reach a state of firmness and inner security. Extend your patience, your understanding, your tolerance and your capacity to forgive. That way your heart will get bigger and become more generous.

On occasions, there are situations that make you suffer and you will have to make important decisions: leave the situation, accept it or change it. Many times, out of fear and a lack of courage, we accept the situation with resignation, we do not accept it from the heart and we continue to suffer. For example, if you accept that you are here with that person (or in that specific situation) and to continue to suffer, you should ask yourself if it is worth paying that price to carry on with them, or, if not, change situation, or change the situation. Sometimes it can be changed, sometimes not; you can control and define your own change, but not that of another person. So you can decide to go somewhere else or change, but do not stop seeking and applying a solution. It is not worth continuing to feed suffering.

The inner strength that you need to take that step is that of loving yourself and thus free yourself without guilt or unnecessary suffering. Freeing the mind is a matter of love, purely a matter of love. Out of love you understand, you accept, you face and you change. Sometimes the incapacity to adapt oneself to change is such that a trauma takes place. What is trauma, and why is it experienced? Trauma is the incapacity of a person to adapt quickly enough to the perceived change.

Change or the idea of change is an external aspect. The person perceives that something is happening and does not feel capable of adapting themselves to the speed at which they perceive it is happening. It can be this, or generally, it is a perceived danger, a situation that threatens their security, stability or identity. They have the fear or worry of some loss and feel that they cannot adapt quickly enough. This is not a logical process; it is a process that takes place, in general, in the subconscious.

The incapacity to adapt oneself to change produces traumas. Sometimes the trauma can be so deeply inside the soul that it only resurges years later, in the form of a blockage or trauma, when the person receives some stimuli from the outside and, suddenly, feels incapable of facing up to them, in an inexplicable way. Trauma is an incapacity to adapt or to change to the rhythm or level required of the perceived change or the threat they are feeling. On the occasions that this happens, they need to be offered psychological help to free themselves of the trauma and to live fully free of the inner fears.

Shining

In order to shine you have to live out the authenticity of your being, live in love, serenity and freedom. To find the authenticity of your being you do not need formulas of doctrine, but rather a strong heart, capable of renouncing its "programming" and its selfishness; a heart that has nothing to protect and nothing to be ambitious about and that, therefore, leaves the mind free and without fear, in search of the truth; a heart that is always prepared to accept new information and change its mind.

A heart like that ends up turning into a lamp that dissipates the darkness that envelops the body of humanity. If all human beings were gifted with a similar heart, Anthony de Mello reminds us in *The Way to Love*: "They would no longer see themselves as "communists", as "capitalists", as "Christians", "Muslims" or "Buddhists", but rather their own far-sightedness would make them see that all their thoughts, concepts and beliefs are turned off lights, signs of their ignorance. And, on seeing it, the limits of their respective ponds would disappear, and they would find themselves flooded by the ocean that joins all human beings in truth".

In that state and with a heart like that, the love that flows from us in all directions, embracing both strangers and friends, family members and acquaintances, is the highest of all, and the most authentic expression of the spirit. Original love, the purest, is the love of God, divine love, which is not selfish or conditional.

There is pain that is only healed with the experience of that love. Your soul needs a massage for it to dissolve and melt all the tension that has brought about the pain. To meditate is to love and open yourself to spiritual love, whereby the fears vanish and the courage emerges to be the shining, tender and marvellous being that you are.

It is in that state of free consciousness when your being shines like a lighthouse of light. A freedom in which there is not attachment, there are not ties, there is not fear, there are no blockages, barriers, repression, oppression.

That freedom is only possible if we return to that state of original purity of being. Purity, a word we do not use much in our shared language, means, without stains, without marks, mixtures, imperfections, that is, the original pure state, as you are, transparent, a being of light, without all the pollution that has entered your mind and your heart throughout your existence. In meditation we go beyond those defences to go to the heart of being, to go to that sacred space that has remained unharmed by suffering, pollution, fear and negativity.

There are many mental, emotional and physical consequences of fear. Fear is an inner enemy that prevents us from shining and being ourselves. It doesn't make it easy for us to express the authentic beauty of our being and communicate in a fluid and easy way. Fear makes us repress and not express the most beautiful part of our personality. We are afraid to show the feelings that are susceptible to being attacked or ridiculed by others.

It is knowing yourself, your true being, that will help you to overcome that fear of shining. The knowledge of your being includes the knowledge of your origin, your origin as a spiritual being. The origin, the present and the destination. The destination we create with our daily actions, with our thoughts. The one who can change their thoughts can change their destination, as the American Civil War novelist Stephen Crane tells us.You need an apprenticeship, and to carry out some inner work of strengthening so that, when there is a loss, you can accompany that person in the process of their death; when there is a disappointment, you can forgive yourself and forgive; when the company does not work like before, you can accumulate new learning to make it be more effective in the contemporary world.

That is, find creative solutions, but do not let go of your state of wholeness that encompasses love, peace, serenity, joy, happiness and gratitude. Move from the culture of complaint to that of gratitude. Your mental state changes so much, from when you are complaining to when you show gratitude! Your vibration changes, the expression on your face and your inner wellbeing. Live in gratitude and it will be easier to keep shining and glowing.

You Choose: Being, State of Being and Doing

It is essential to reaffirm that, fundamentally, you are a good human being and that you have a choice of what you want to think, say and do. You choose how you are, how you feel and what you do. You have the power to choose whether your response will be positive or negative, passive or active, indifferent or attentive.

On what do you base yourself to choose and make decisions? There are different factors that limit your power to make a free choice. These factors are limitations that arise from existing habits and from the influences of people that dominate your thinking, your attitudes, preconceptions, etc. You are also limited by the influence of your own fears, desires or lack of clarity. The more you practise positive thinking and meditation, the more you will free yourself of those limiting factors.

What are the influences that push us towards one direction or another? Many people are not used to thinking for themselves or even prefer to go along with what others think and say. Courage is required to sit down calmly, quiet, and think about the ethical choices before you, make a considered evaluation and make a decision.

As you pass through your childhood and youth, you acquire preconceptions from your social and cultural environment; that is why you come to think that some things are always positive and others are always negative when, in fact, they can be neutral.

Whose is the choice? Who chooses how you are? Are you going to be frustrated and dominated by your fears, or are you going to shine and share all the beauty of your being. Being happy is a decision, a responsibility and a right of all human beings.

From today on you will not allow your husband or wife, or children, grandmothers, or grandfathers, or parents-in-law, or business partners, or secretaries, anybody, to eliminate your inner shining. In the end, that way they will be happier; perhaps not at first, because a power game is created.

When someone dominates you, they control you and make you feel frustrated, feel bad, they satisfy their own ego like that by submitting you to their influence. You should decide whether you want to become the one who satisfies the egos of others by being their victim. It is not a very healthy attitude, but we fall prey to that game.

Get back your personal governance and do not be afraid to be free and responsible for your choices. You are free to the extent that you are more responsible for how you are and how you feel.

In meditation you can revise everything that has influenced you and know how to clean it, so that only the highest, the most positive, and the most beautiful influences you. This depends on each one of us. In this world of today everything is on offer, from the most negative, violent, corrupt, low and mediocre, to the purest, highest and most spiritual. It depends on each one what they want to consume and what they want to make of their life and how to focus it.

Meditation helps you to choose well, to strengthen what you want and to work on that positive vision of yourself, to reconcile yourself with your past, to know how to forgive, to know how to accept, to tolerate, flow and strengthen yourself. All these values, virtues and powers will help you to shine.

When what you are, how you are and what you do are in line, your being shines with all its strengths and you transmit the joy of being alive in all your expressions and actions.

Sometimes a situation causes you unhappiness and makes it difficult to stay joyful. At that moment you can ask yourself: "What is this situation teaching me?" "What can I improve in myself in order not to recreate or relive this problem?" "What can I bring to the situation?" These questions generate positive answers that lead you to love, generosity, forgiveness, patience and learning.

Avoid, at the same time, the questions that increase your unhappiness and draw a curtain in front of your being that reduces or hides your shining such as: "Why have I had to go through this?" "Why has it happened to me?" "How dare they?" "Who do they think I am?" These questions only cause answers of anxiety, rejection, hate, bitterness and aggression.

Ask Yourself: What Do You Want?

In the day-to-day you can have different desires and want different things: what you want for today; what you want to do at the weekend; what you want to achieve with your professional career; the results that you want to get this year; what relationships you want to focus on. But, at bottom, what is your purpose? What are you doing here? What do you want? Where do you want to go and how far do you want to get?

When you open yourself within to answer these questions, you will see that the inner voice that answers you is the voice of your own consciousness and is connected to some value: what you want is to discover how to live in the truth and not appearances, what you want is to live in and from love, what you want is to be free, you want peace.

If you listen to and follow this voice, you will come close to your wholeness, because you will align your energies: your vision, your intention, your motivation, your consciousness, with your action and your life. Each morning, on looking at yourself in the mirror, ask yourself: "If today was the last day of my life, would I want to do what I am about to do?" And if for various days in a row the answer has been "no", then it is a sign that you have to change something, given that your action is not aligned with your purpose.

What our being wants and seeks at bottom is connected to living some values in an authentic way in all areas of life. What happens is that we have disconnected from our true, original and authentic spiritual life, and we live the day-to-day from our defences and our fears. So we do things only from a sense of duty and compulsive perfectionism, which mutilates the imagination, sensitivity, spontaneity, and the pleasure of savouring the path of human action.

We have to decide that we want to have time. The decision to have time for human tasks like playing, reading, thinking, reflecting, learning, meditating, ordering ideas, having friends, loving or simply being is essential in order to give meaning to life. It has to be facilitated on a practical level from the different degrees of power and management that each person has in life. Don't wait for someone to magically appear to make you happy. You have to know that nobody will come as if by magic to rescue you from your essential emptiness. It has to be you yourself who decides to live with a purpose and fill yourself in order to overcome your deficiencies and enjoy your life.

Depression
This is not a book about depression, but it is worth mentioning it,

given that it is the antithesis of shining. You feel depressed when you lack happiness and optimism about the possibilities that you have and a constantly negative consciousness and vision is produced. You lose hope. In depression you lack an interest in things. You are sensitive to criticisms, even if they are minimal. You feel sadness, impatience, a lack of perspectives. You try to reach satisfaction through material means, like, for example, eating too much, eating sweet things, etc.

You get depressed because you remember past errors; because you need the experience of love in life; out of the habit of seeing only the negative in each situation, without perceiving that a positive side exists. The imagination is fertile in a negative sense: debilitating, depressing and even destructive. Nothing seems attractive to you and you feel unmotivated.

To get out of this state it is important to accept yourself; keep a mental state of detached observer; don't allow the mind to cling to depressing thoughts and tune it into the positive aspects of life. Sometimes negativity and weakness have overwhelmed you to such a point that in order to get out of that state you need a "bombardment" of positivism: go on a spiritual retreat; surround yourself by good company; attend a course of personal development; get out of that state in which you are closed into yourself. Take the step. Nobody can do it for you.

BLISS

He that is not happy with little will not be so with a lot.
Lao Tse

The state of wholeness takes you to a state of bliss, of happiness, of tranquillity, of harmony, wellbeing, love; it is a state in which you feel light, you feel yourself flow, you feel inwardly free. You don't feel a weight, heaviness, suffocated, stress. On the contrary, you feel ethereal like light, luminous like an angel, positive.

You realize and are conscious that you are the creator of your thoughts and feelings; that a thought can block your capacity to feel yourself whole, full, realized and a thought can lead you to sadness or to being irritated. A single thought can be the key to opening the door to feel the values of being. It has to be a pure thought, potent, clear and concentrated.

Appreciate and enjoy the present. The present is the gift that you have here and now. Enjoy it. Stop complaining and begin to appreciate and value what you have. You cannot force either people or situations to fulfil your desires. Revise your expectations, desires and projections. Respect the space and freedom of action of each one. This dissolves fears, will reduce anxiety and will help you to enjoy the present.

Live looking straight at reality and don't cling on to anything. If you didn't cling on to anything, if you didn't fear to lose anything, you would be free to flow like the mountain torrent. Always fresh, alive and changing.

Acquire a taste for the new, change and uncertainty; only thus will your fear of losing the familiar and known disappear, and you will expect and receive the new and unknown with excitement. This is the base from which to enjoy this present moment. Living in the present is one of the best ways to overcome worries and fears.

Recognize that almost always now everything is fine. It doesn't matter how bad or painful you think something is going to be, life is almost always fine in this instant. For most of our lives, what causes us pain and fear is our expectation that there is going to be more damage and fear in the future. Revising at any moment this instant with the question "Is everything fine now in your life?" we discover that, invariably, the answer is a rotund "yes".

As you develop your skill of being in the present instant, it can be a good experience to return to something that you feared in the past, with your new present consciousness.

Enjoy from the silence.

Calm your mind. Listen to yourself. Treat your self with affection. Don't force yourself. Generate thoughts full of beauty that motivate and enthuse you. In silence you strengthen yourself to relate to others without defences and without fears. If you work to achieve it, you will perceive the state of wholeness that we can all reach.

THE SACRED

Recently I was in the National Archaeological Museum of Greece, in Athens. One of the things that I could see is the sacred element that there was in the life of ancient civilisations that has been lost today. We live in a superficiality in which we eat, we talk, and we act in a way that is ordinary, vulgar, and superficial, with much noise.

The sacred element of the way of nourishing ourselves has been lost. In relationships, in how we live, how we walk, in everything, we have forgotten that divine and sacred energy. All that has become vulgar and ordinary.

The ancient civilizations asked permission of the gods before using the resources of nature. Water, for example, was considered a precious and sacred resource, creator and sustainer of life. That respect of the resources that nature provides us with has been lost.

Our body, made up of the elements of nature, of water in the main part, is the temple of the energy of our being. However, we do not inhabit our bodies with the respect that living in a temple implies. The body has become a resonance box where our blockages manifest themselves: anxieties, fears and anguishes, even in the rubbish bin where we throw corpses (meat), smoke (tobacco), and an endless list of polluting and unnecessary substances.

The connection with spiritual and divine energy helps you to reach wholeness.

Where do you begin? By respecting your body. Treating it as a temple. Caring for your mind. Meditating. Learn to channel the energy of your being, that is, the energy of your thought and feeling, in a positive direction that helps you to express yourself from your highest state.

Rise from a negative state or, if not negative, from a vulgar and ordinary state to an intuitive and spiritual state that is even beyond the rational and mental. That is, a state in which you free the energy of your love, your being, your peace and express it. Instead of expressing irritation, complaints, criticism, negativity, you express appreciation, valuing, and positivism. That change depends on you. It is a question of doing inner work. You can begin with meditation, reflection and knowledge of yourself.

Meditation serves to strengthen you and lift up, thus sublimating, your energy. We have the example of the snake that, with the melody of the music, gets up and ascends. In some Egyptian sphinxes and in other cultures too, they represent the cobra lifted up at the centre of the forehead, which symbolises the energy of the soul that on the one hand can be dragged along the ground, like the snake, but that rises and is elevated with the melody of divine wisdom. That of the snake is a good symbol: it is an animal that has that capacity to rise up and ascend on hearing the melody of music. The human being can rise up and enjoy the "nectar of the heavens" on listening to and internalising the wisdom.

HOPE

Hope is the dream of a waking man.
Aristotle

Living with hope keeps us awake. With hope we are open to the opportunities that life offers us. We overcome fear and expect the best. With hope our forces are joined in order to deal with and overcome difficulties. We maintain the vision that everything will get better and things will channel themselves, giving out benefits to all. Hope helps us to keep the meaning of our life alive.

In the midst of the constant changes of life and confusing or chaotic situations, hope helps us to keep afloat and not to drown in the whirlwind that at times causes unexpected or sudden changes. Without hope, we expect the worst. Our vision gets cloudy; we do not find or see any ray of light to see by. The mind fills with questions, allowing itself to be obfuscated by doubts and insecurity. Fear takes control of us and everything turns into a mountain or an insurmountable wall. It seems to us that we will not be able to get out of the difficult and critical moments, or it will be difficult for us to get out of the "hole". We feel incapable of going forward. Fear and doubt paralyse us and prevent us from deciding with clarity and acting with determination. We need to find support or help and, when we don't get it, we go even further down.

When we feel ourselves to be surrounded by violence, suffering and pain, we find it difficult to sustain hope. We need to understand the causes of that suffering, to go to the root that brings it into being, since only thus will we be able to keep the light of hope on. Understand that pain is a sign that indicates to us that something has to change. If your molar didn't hurt you wouldn't go to the dentist nor would you realize that something in your teeth isn't working. In the same way, emotional and mental pain suggests to us that something is not right. Understanding the signs that that suffering brings us helps us to accept the causes of the pain and to generate the power to transform it. Out of understanding, acceptance and being willing to change, we relieve the pain and keep hope alive.

In spite of all the international, national, local, family and personal conflicts that there may be, **there are many positive things to be happy about**. There are more and more people aware of the importance of personal development, and of taking care of oneself on a physical, emotional, mental and spiritual level. There is a list of positive things and situations to be happy about. Be grateful for and discover the benefit that there is behind everything that happens. All of it helps you to strengthen hope in yourself, in others and in humanity.

Hope is the base from which to trust and have enthusiasm and motivation in all we do. Hope strengthens trust in life and in that beauty and truth are possible. Hope and trust go together; without hope it is difficult to trust and without trust it is difficult to sustain hope. Revise your beliefs, since there are some beliefs that lead you to despair. For example, when you believe that the worst can always happen; when you believe that others have the intention to hurt you or when you believe that you are no good and will be rejected. These beliefs debilitate your capacity to trust and make you lose hope.

If you believe in the inherent goodness of the human being, you open yourself to trust and to hope that the best of each person can emerge, and thus create healthy relationships, live with wholeness and, in sum, create a better world.

Discover and trust in your inner resources; you have a great capacity for adaptation, tolerance, flexibility, courage and serenity, which arise out of the understanding of yourself and of allowing yourself to be who you are, without complexes or blockages that prevent you from doing so. If your actuation is motivated by love, gratitude, peace, trust, co-operation and solidarity, you generate a positive energy that attracts the positive to you. Enthusiasm and hope are awakened in you: you are freeing yourself of the paralysing energy of fear, you are opening yourself to be yourself, your creativity flows and you feel strong to accept, face and change.

You create the future basing yourself on what you think, feel and do in the present. If you act responding to your values, it is easy for you **to trust in your destiny**. That strengthens your hope that all will go well, and, if not, you know and trust your inner resources to be able to deal with things and change. That trust feeds the enthusiasm, the motor energy that, with motivation and passion, helps us to advance.

When you stop feeling love, when you lose courage and you feel weak, when you feel insecure and do not see with clarity where to go towards, **hope lights the way for you** to carry on going forward. If you fall, get up again and carry on looking ahead. Don't look back. Don't let your past be a burden that is too heavy and prevents you from advancing. Focus your vision on your objective and on all your potential to achieve it.

Whatever happens, keep the lamp of hope lit. You can. You will achieve it. Change will become reality. You will free yourself from the shadows of fears, blockages and the other limitations that debilitate you.

Live each situation as an opportunity. Learn from criticism and failures. On living life as a constant opportunity for personal growth and learning, you keep hope always alive.

Give yourself moments of silence on beginning each day, during the day and on finishing the day, to connect with the essential of your being. That way your awareness stays awake, living out your hope, your motivation and your values.

With enthusiasm, hope and bravery you can achieve great objectives in your life.

MEDITATION

Every day we have the opportunity to learn, heal, love, enjoy and see the inherent goodness of others. When we forget these things, we are contaminated by stress and fears. How to remember all this when it seems that there is so much to do and so much negativity to deal with? The theory is inspiring, but, how to apply it in order to achieve all those objectives? By learning to nourish our being.

You nourish your being by going to the depths of silence and learning to love yourself and appreciate yourself. Devoting a time to this will bring about the change in how you do things and in your attitudes and habits. You will begin to see as well an improvement in your relationships and the quality of your life. By adopting a systematic practice, you can make the changes that you desire in your life, or if not the old models of behaviour and habits and the influences of the world will diminish the power and efficacy of your efforts, like the tide that takes with it the sandcastle on the beach.

It is important that you create a space of silence, not only in your mind but also in your home and, if possible, at your place of work. In many companies and hospitals in different countries, rooms for silence and meditation are being created. If at home you don't have a room for it, you can create "the corner of silence", that you will only use for this end. In that space you will have the opportunity to prepare the day each morning and, in the evening or at night, unload your mind of the useless thoughts or feelings that you may have accumulated.

The regular practice of meditation allows you to enter into contact with the immutable essence of your being, with the best of you, the purest essential instance of your nature. It is an experience of serenity and concentration that is essential for the construction of an authentic self-esteem, security and trust in yourself and in others. Meditation helps you to recognize and understand your true, original and authentic identity, as a metaphysical energy, a spiritual energy, which is the base of elevated thinking.

The inner discipline of practicing meditation is necessary. The mind needs to relax and refresh itself if you want to feel yourself positive and strong in order to live each day with serenity and efficacy. When you recognize this, you will give personal priority to the daily practice of inner silence.

Meditate to Be Aware

In meditation you learn to see yourself as conscious of your being as a soul, a star, as a concentrated energy that moves the body and is the essential and energetic source of your life. It is the energy of the conscious being, it thinks, feels and remembers. It is the energy that expresses itself through the body.

Meditation gives you the opportunity to strengthen the vision to see yourself as a free being. For this vision to take hold in reality, you have to overcome what prevents you from believing in it: the fear of freedom, the fear of true love, the fear of accepting responsibility. The fear is such that we are even afraid of positive things. We fear to get rid of our defences to open ourselves to beauty and to the most marvellous things that life offers us and that emerge from the purity of our being.

For meditation to be effective in the change of beliefs and habits, knowledge is required, and more concretely the knowledge of being. You have to begin to know yourself and know how the energy of your thought works, how the mechanism of your creative mind works and be capable of having it under your control. Thinking well is a personal choice.[18] Dominate your inner energies by knowing how they work. The energy of your being is the source of all trauma, fear and violence and it is also the source of all the great beauty that there is in you and in all creation.

Meditation is an essential inner exercise where you relearn to choose and control your states of awareness. Meditation helps you to generate the space of silence necessary for you to realize who you are, how you are, what is happening to you, your reactions and the speed at which you think. Realizing is the first step towards transformation.

One of the effects of meditation is to bring about realisations in which you become aware of the things that are going on inside you. Sometimes we use the expression "They don't know what they are doing", referring to someone who is acting in an immoral or amoral way. Being aware and being awake in order to realize the implication and consequences of your actions is the best deterrent to not acting in an inappropriate way.

The small voice of the conscience brings that state of "awakening" and of "realizing". Because in meditation you feel tranquil and focus your thoughts inwards; in that state, one perceives the sound of the voice of the conscience. It is a voice that is not affected by material worries or the concern for image and public appearance. You are not distracted by activities, noise, loose thoughts, mental chatter and all the things that distance you from the contact with your true being. You can listen within yourself.

Observe

Observe your own thoughts. Affirm the positive energy through the repetition of positive images and thoughts of yourself. Recognize and appreciate the positive feelings that arise from there. Don't be passive or submissive, but rather active, positive and aware in all your responses. Observe how you involve yourself in situations, how they influence you. From observation you should become aware of how you are.

This exercise helps you to keep aware, to protect yourself in the case that it is necessary, to not be influenced and to stay relaxed and serene. Out of serenity, you can make more correct decisions and act with greater clarity.

Meditate to Calm Yourself and Concentrate

Of the 30,000 thoughts (or more) that your mind generates every day, more than half are useless, unnecessary, superficial, trivial, ordinary, and as well there will be the odd one that is negative and even destructive.

On beginning meditation you first learn to relax. Once you know how to relax quickly and easily, the following step is knowing how to focus your mind and concentrate it. That way you learn to acquire the art of thinking little, thinking well, thinking with quality, thinking in an elevated way, thinking meaningfully and usefully.

Concentration is the base from which to achieve good results in all areas of your life. Meditation helps you to create that state in which your mind stays concentrated and focussed. From that state you connect to the inner part of your being and go past the defences generated by anguish, fear, pain, worries; you go past all the superficial identities that label you and box you into a specific role. You go past them and reach the inner part, the heart of your soul, and there you can listen to yourself without being distracted. You stay focused.

Visualize
A study shows that the majority of athletes who win at the Olympics work on visualization, months before, they saw themselves having achieved their goal. Visualization helped them to believe in themselves. The efforts made with this energy have a greater probability of success than when you make the effort without trusting in what you are doing and without seeing yourself as achieving your objectives.

If you think about your frustrations from yesterday, you stop believing in yourself and get more frustrated. Visualisation is worked at from the present towards the future, without allowing the burdens from the past to condition you. You visualize yourself as a person who has already overcome their fears, their bad habits and that is transformed. You see yourself already in transformation, already "I am a being of peace", not "I am going to become a being of peace", I am already a being of light, I am already an angel.

The power of that vision – you believe in positive affirmations towards your being – is such that it helps you to generate a metamorphosis; not a small change, but a radical change, because you make it easy for the sleeping being that you are to emerge and show itself. You stop always expecting the worst and hope for and visualise the best.

What we do in meditation is to invoke, recreate, visualize our being as free from all the defences we have covered ourselves with. In meditation you feel that state free of all of that. In practice you have to work so that what you have felt, visualised and lived in that time of silence you can express in action and you can live it in the day-to-day of your relationships, without defences and without fears. It is a question of overcoming mental and emotional laziness in order to make a personal effort in that direction.

Visualize yourself as a peaceful being, free and unblocked. Visualize yourself in your habitual relationships and circumstances. Begin the day with an exercise of visualization in order to prepare yourself to live a day full of healthy energy.

Listen in the Silence

In meditation you connect to the experience of silence whereby both the mind and the heart are calmed. The mental chatter stops. A gentle flow of slow, clear, luminous and peaceful thought is produced. The organs of the senses and the body are calmed and your emotions are peaceful. From this state you can listen to the voice of your conscience, the voice that guides you. That way you awaken the divine intuition.

On listening to that voice, you are strengthened. In this way you start to align your life with your purpose, with what you really want. You begin to have more determination to carry out the things that you really want to do, without fear preventing it.

With meditation you learn to love the silence. A tender, beautiful and sweet silence. That way you value each word more, given that to not lose that experience of the sweet silence, you try to talk less, to speak with sweetness and gentleness. When you generate the love and pleasure in going to the silence, it helps you express the best of yourself.

To help others, sometimes it is better not to speak, not to use words; to use the vibration of your thoughts and good feelings that emerge from that state of silence. That way you will enter the hearts that are trapped in darkness. Those hearts are in darkness, they have lost hope, and they are hurt, wounded, discouraged.

From your silence you transmit to them the light with which they can find a way out.

To receive it, they have to be willing. But if it is still not their time, at least they will know that there are people willing to help from a silence that does not judge, does not complain. A silence that accepts, appreciates and loves, generating an atmosphere in which one can be oneself and feel free to change at their own pace, without feeling forced or coerced, but rather from understanding and love.

Meditate to Cleanse Profoundly

When you are capable of relaxing, controlling your thought and concentrating, you can reach deeper and more subtle states of meditation from which you connect with your potential for peace and purest love and on the other hand, you clean out unnecessary memories. You reach the spiritual power that allows you to transform habits that are not very healthy and the beliefs that sustain them. Out of love and peace you can purify and clarify the turbulent waters that there are at times in the subconscious. When you meditate, you review whether there is something that has influenced you and you clean it out, so that only the highest, the most positive, the most beautiful, comes out of you.

Meditation and reflection help you to clean out the register that, from the subconscious, brings about inadequate thoughts and uncontrolled emotions. Cleansing in depth requires a clear purpose, being prepared to let go of the past; cleansing the wounds and pain accumulated in the store of your being; facing the present with dignity, with wisdom and visualizing a future full of trust and wholeness. The first thing that meditation teaches us is to cleanse the mind of the useless thoughts that it creates in the present moment. While your mind believes this kind of thoughts, it will not be able to concentrate. And if it cannot concentrate, it will not be able to cleanse in depth.

Meditation helps you to live through that inner process without pain. From a space of love, you feel secure in order to open up the cupboards of your being. Do not open them before, because the accumulated pain can be overwhelming and the loneliness experienced can terrify you. Because you are alone, with yourself, with your past and with your present, and you are alone here, with your cupboards and your files. In the silence of contemplative meditation you feel that the divine energy accompanies you and helps you to overcome the fear of loneliness. You feel embraced by an energy and the presence of unconditional love that accepts you as you are.

Meditate to Heal and Let Go

Meditation is the process of healing the inner wounds produced by the two main illusions or mirages that influence being: in the first place, that we are only physical beings and, secondly, that love and happiness can only be reached through the physical senses. When we allow these illusions to have an influence on our actions, we go against the essence of being and leave an impression (*sanskara*) on our consciousness.

During meditation we let go of these mirages and thus a spiritual healing takes place: there is a rediscovery and a realisation of the truth of who we are and what we are that frees our spiritual energy and restores the consciousness of the soul, of being. Thus is restored the natural nature of the soul that is not to take, but rather to give. With the practice of meditation you learn to develop the skill of letting go of negative experiences accumulated from the past, to dissolve blockages, calm tensions and to generate inner clarity.

Meditation helps not only to heal the soul, but also physically, the impact that the experiences of pain have left on your body are erased. This happens with the practice of deep meditation. Not with a relaxation of a few minutes nor with a superficial meditation. It is the experience of deep meditation that will help you to heal your soul completely of accumulated fears, pains and grief. On letting go of the baggage of the past, the fears that you have in the present caused by the experiences of the past will disappear. Simply let go of it, don't question, and don't re-live that situation in your mind even once.

Meditation opens you to a process of learning in which you learn to take care of your heart and mind, your capacity to feel and think, in such a way that you keep your mind serene, clear, and your heart strong, without fear or pain. When your feelings go from one place to another and your thoughts too, you lose control over your inner world and over your most valuable resources. Then, your life goes off the rails and you begin to act in an uncontrolled way and to generate habits that are not very healthy.

To meditate is to care for your mind and strengthen your heart in order to live a fuller and more satisfactory life. Strengthen yourself to be happier, and for your life to have more meaning. In meditation you can go beyond the merely sensorial reality and reach another real spiritual dimension. But this is only possible when you learn to detach yourself, which means to abandon accumulated negative habits, emotional tendencies and negative memories. On this journey, it is guaranteed that you will lose your baggage!

In any case, I should make clear that meditation is not a therapy. Meditation is transforming, but it is not a therapy as such. It should never be used as an alternative to therapy. Therapy is necessary for some people whose patterns of thought and behaviour are compulsive, addictive, out of control, traumatic. Some people need therapy before they can practice meditation in order to get satisfactory results. When they try to meditate, the volume and power of their thoughts is so strong, so crushing, that they feel overwhelmed, flooded by these negative impressions. That person may need to have sessions with a therapist to help them discover the roots of the traumas that they carry within. The therapist can help them to become aware with care and little by little. Then they will be ready for meditation.

Meditate to Accept

The mistake that usually takes place in western society is that we want to change people. It is a very strong habit in us. We focus on the change that others have to make and we forget that what is really in our hands is to change ourselves. We want to "save" or change others. We even see this in our response to international assistance. We try to save people. It is good to save lives, but we have to be aware that we have the attitude of saviours. Our help is from that attitude of saving the other, as if we were a superior race. Accepting the other is to accept that they live by following a style, conditions, beliefs and attitude in the face of life that are different to ours.

Each person generates their own reality. Therefore, we cannot impose on our children or loved ones that they generate a reality that we would like. We can inspire, motivate, enthuse, but each one creates their own inner world and their own external reality.

From a state of contemplative meditation you learn to accept with an open and generous heart:

* You accept that the other is different.
* You accept that they do not always act as you would like.
* You accept that situations come and go.
* You accept your physical, mental and emotional condition.
* You accept yourself.

You understand that you create your destiny and you can inspire others to create a good destiny. But you know that it is in their hands to create the destiny that they decide to.

Accepting means taking on your aloneness. Because it is you alone, with yourself, with your past and with your present.

Sometimes we flee from ourselves, we hide behind action, doing, schedules, projects and journeys. We live a life of superficiality, of distraction and noise. With outer noise, we silence the inner noise, we turn it down, and it is less heard. It is like when the neighbours make a noise – we turn the television up so as not to hear them. We put the volume of action up very high and we do not listen to our inner voice. We flee from the silence because we are fleeing from aloneness. It is in solitude where you can really see yourself, become aware, reflect and transform yourself.

Accepting is not to flee from reality. Reality here and now, and universal reality. To meditate is not to flee, to meditate is to face and live reality, but to live it with wholeness. I do not understand being realistic as the limits that we impose on ourselves on seeing reality in the here and now, but rather being realistic with all our potential to create, change and improve. For some, this is being utopian. If we forget our creative potential we will succumb to the limits imposed by our minds and our beliefs and we will stop dreaming and creating a better world.

Acceptance undoes your system of opposing resistance, which means you save a lot of energy, you keep strong and from that strength you can change. Remember that accepting does not mean necessarily being in agreement. Accepting is not to be submissive. The resistances that we have to accepting others, situations and changes consume a great part of our mental and emotional energy. Meditation helps you to re-establish your inner balance.

Meditate to Transform Habits

At the heart of being there is a spiritual energy, pure, of peace, love, truth and happiness without dependence. Being aware and experiencing this energy provides you with the inner strength necessary for change. Meditation is the method of access in order to allow that energy to come to the surface of your consciousness and in your mind in order to colour your thoughts and feelings. In a way very similar to that of a volcano whose melted lava, hot, flows from the centre of the Earth to the surface, we, on meditating, can create volcanoes of power.

You can do an exercise, a meditation whereby you choose a

habit that you don't want, and you will replace it with a characteristic that you would like to incorporate, like a thread, into the cloth
of your personality. For example, replace impatience with
patience. You can do a meditation following the thoughts indicated
in the meditation at the end of this chapter with this theme: change
a habit.

Meditate to Renew Yourself

Meditation is an internal process of renewal and liberation. When
you control the process of moving through the states of
consciousness (choose, detach yourself and go beyond), you get
back the spiritual power, which was trapped or hidden.You learn
to channel your energy in order to unblock yourself. You control
better what you think and you think better. You free your being of
bad feelings, bad energies and bad influences.

On the one hand, you have to learn to generate positivism; on
the other, you have to learn to protect yourself from energies that
are unhealthy, sick, atrophying, on an emotional level. Meditation
helps to do this, to digest situations when they have to be digested
and not to consume what they offer when it is not necessary; if you
know that something will make you ill, you don't eat it. On the
level of relationships, you learn not to allow certain situations,
scenes or words to influence you. That way you stay renewed and
your energy flows without blockages.

Awakening and Loving

On meditating you awaken and mobilize your own spiritual
qualities. You begin to be more affectionate, more tender, free of
defences of fear, arrogance, and you are the first to experience the
spiritual love that bursts out from within you towards the outside.

From the silence you open yourself to the experience of true
love, pure love, love free of attachments, dependences and fears.
Imagine a love like that. That love is glory, happiness, wholeness.
You become aware of what arises from within, and you stop
looking for it outside. You awaken to the reality of your potential

for love.

In relationships we find a creative opportunity to express our peacefulness, our feelings of love and joy, reverting thus the direction of the flow of energy of our life from the outside inwards. We begin to share from the inside out.

We realize that when we feel fuller is when we express all our love and creativity by sharing it with others. Then, each action becomes a painting, a sculpture, a work of art. Each action leaves an impact of spontaneous beauty and creativity. It is transformed into something that people recognize as an act driven by the love of life, generator of positive changes in which one dares to be and to shine.

God, the transcendent connection
We need a shower of positivism in order to fill ourselves with positive energy. For this, we have to connect with the ocean of positivism, that is, with God. God is a being that is totally positive, totally pacific, unconditionally loving. All religions say that God is love. When we connect with the energy of God, we feel a bath of positivism.

We are accustomed to connecting with the energy of God to ask him to solve our matters: "This is what is happening to me: my husband is ill, let God cure him", "Let's see if God helps my son to behave better" and "This is happening, let's see if God does something". God does not intervene in our karmas, our karmic relationships or in our exchange with human beings. A karmic bond is when you generate a dependency with someone. Each one has created their reality and it is out of laziness, ignorance and weakness that we want to get God to change it when we do not like it.

God gives us the power for our values to emerge, be strengthened and become virtues and power that help us to accept, face, change and live by applying creative solutions in the day-to-day. God offers us a clean mirror so that we can become aware of who we are and the reality of what happens to us. So that we can see and discern what is false from what is authentic. You strengthen yourself and you can free yourself and be transformed thanks to the divine spiritual power. In meditation, you receive and feel the power of God. The language of God emerges from the silence of your mind and in the harmony of your being.

Meditation offers you the possibility of establishing communication and a relationship with the Supreme Being. In a meditative state you can channel that divine energy. The opening of this channel to establish the connection, you can achieve, and soon.

On your willingness to change depends both the cleanliness of your subconscious, the transformation of deeply-rooted beliefs and habits that have become vices that I have spoken of in previous chapters, and the overcoming of weaknesses and blockages; that is, it requires your effort. When you take the step, the energy of God helps you and makes the work easier that otherwise would be more difficult.

In the same way that as human beings we have parents and we maintain a relationship with them, as spiritual beings, God is our Supreme Father and Mother. Meditation helps us to get back this relationship and that connection with the experience and feeling of belonging to something more than just the sensorial and physical reality that we see in the day-to-day. Our selfishness has left us orphans of divinity and the sacred. With meditation we can get back this sense of belonging.

Return

In meditation you can return to the dimension from which your soul proceeds, which I would call the return home, to your original essence, to your home. This journey home is not a flight from reality but rather the return to a superior reality.

The unreality for the soul is the belief that the physical world is all that exists and that happiness always requires some physically stimulated experience.

In your home of light and silence, of peace and liberation, live your Father and Mother, God, the Supreme Being. This home has been called by many names, such as: the land of Nirvana (beyond sound), the Brahmlok (the world of the energy of subtle and spiritual light, the Brahm), Muktidham (the dwelling place of liberation)...

Daily Practice

Meditation has to be practiced on a daily basis if we want to achieve satisfactory results. We have had bad, negative and fearful thoughts for a long time. We cannot transform them with just a few sporadic sessions of meditation. It is good to meditate every day for a time, in the morning and at night, to start cleansing. You go along accumulating things within you, often without realising. Therefore, you have to cleanse as you go along. In order to heal, relax, strengthen, it is good to do it regularly. It is simple; it is just a question of deciding to do it. In the same way that you eat every day, you learn to nourish your spirit by meditating. The time that you devote to meditation you get back because it increases your concentration, focus, clarity and determination in action. So you cannot use the excuse that you don't have time.

Think about establishing a practice of regular meditation. You can also learn to meditate in movement and to maintain a peaceful state during the day in action. As well as looking for and isolating certain moments to disconnect from action and connect with the energy of silence. If you are going to sit down to meditate, the most powerful and beneficial thing is to do it at a regular time. Establish for yourself a concrete timetable for your meditation and try not to change it, let it be your time reserved for this practice. It is available for you and that is your time of silence, of strengthening, of clarity and healing. Begin each day with silence that is positive, peaceful, powerful, serene, and clear. Before working, having breakfast, before doing anything, go inside yourself for a time. In that space of introversion you can connect with your original spiritual qualities, recharging your inner batteries with positive thoughts for the day that you are beginning. On ending the day you can return to that space of silence and put aside any thought that is negative, useless, weak, connected to the actions and situations that you have lived through. The past has already passed. And send good feelings where they are needed. Connecting with the best of your being helps you to live more consciously, so that you can relate to others with greater serenity, flexibility, value and efficacy.

The daily practice of meditation in order to prepare the day in the morning and to clean and clarify at night keeps the mind healthy. A healthy mind is light, it is focused, and it is not easily distracted or burdened. During the day you can also find moments to enter into a space of inner silence, even if they are short, of a few minutes, and they help you to control the traffic of your mind and redirect thoughts when necessary.

To begin a change, the starting point is knowledge, understanding and becoming aware. It is not possible to begin this journey without some kind of map that indicates the route that we have to follow to not get lost in a sea of thoughts. There are Raja Yoga meditation centres in many countries that offer these maps and help the person to begin with their meditation practice. Information is shared about how the mind works, the power of positivism, spiritual values and the art of effective concentration. All these maps help you to know yourself better and reinforce your self-esteem and happiness.

A Raja Yoga meditation center is a spiritual school where we can learn the art of enjoying a full life; it is a spiritual clinic where we see how to apply the healing medicines of peace, trust, respect and love in our relationships; it is a spiritual family where we realize that each member is unique and has a goodness that should be respected, accepted and appreciated, and that way we do not stay trapped in the fact of focusing on the weaknesses and roles of others. To establish a solid base in the practice of meditation, it is very helpful to do it in a group. With individual practice you maintain your responsibility and stay autonomous. However, without losing this, you can also join in with group practice, valuing and learning from the experiences and perceptions of others. The group dynamic takes us to another level of experience.

Remember that NOW you have the opportunity to create newness in each aspect of your life and your existence.

Coherence and Integrity

Meditation has to be accompanied, on the one hand, by the practice of the motto that "the past is the past"; on the other, by the practice of not consuming what you don't need, be it words, things that you see, whatever it is: if it is really going to influence you negatively or it is going to hurt you, you do not need to consume it. You have to learn to take care of your heart and mind, your capacity to feel and think. Nourish the mind with high thoughts. Nourish the heart with good feelings. Nourish the soul out of the wisdom that emerges from the silence.

To feel the energy and the power of God it is not enough to meditate, but rather you have to be coherent in your life and your actions. All the religions put forward a code of conduct in order to reach spiritual and divine wholeness: don't kill, don't steal, don't lie, live in the truth, authenticity, in non-violence. Live a life of simplicity, not of opulence. On all the spiritual paths a series of principles necessary to reach the realization of God and the spiritual experience, the mystical experience, are proposed.

Meditation will only give us a maximum result when we are coherent in our life; in how we use our mind, our time, our wealth, our body; what exchange do we have with people? A mediocre, corrupt exchange or a high and spiritual exchange? All of this has an influence. In meditation one cannot flee. Meditation helps you to take responsibility; meditation means to open your eyes, these two and the third eye; that is, the eye of intelligence, of discernment, the divine eye, the eye that allows you to understand who you are and the impact of your actions.

Changing those aspects of your life that affect or diminish your ability to control your mind and live with serenity will be helped by the practice of meditation. For example, taking substances that alter your mental state such as alcohol or drugs, seeing violent films or pursuing aims that reinforce your old habits of behaviour and that distance you from your true being. Some changes take place naturally and easily when we incorporate meditation into our life and experience its benefits. Our desires to have material objects beyond those that are necessary for living diminish. A greater respect towards nature flowers in us and we lose the desire to eat animal meat. We become more attentive and selective about the company we keep and the subjects that we talk about; realising that everything we say and do has an impact around us. With all this, your self-esteem and trust increase, you take interest in helping the other, in sharing the benefits that you receive on this inner journey. You life is filled with greater meaning and purpose. Thus, you want to do what is best for you, for your family and for the world.

I invite you to meditate, to reflect and to awaken your inner voice. I propose that you clean out your inner files, clear the turbulent inner waters and overcome fears. I suggest to you that you think less, think better and think positively.

The main thing in your journey is to BEGIN. Accept the challenge to try it, without being sidetracked by excuses, and thus begin the journey. On taking the first steps, success will be waiting for you. Optimism, hope and faith open the horizons of possibilities. You intuit all the good that there can be, although for now perhaps you might not see it.

Thus, between us all, we will create a better world, worthy, without violence, without fear, a world based on trust, respect and love.

PRACTICAL MEDITATIONS

Meditation 1
Discover the Beauty of Being

A meditation to reflect on and experience the original qualities and virtues of the soul. When you are in contact with these treasures, you begin to shine.

Create a space within you. Sit down and go within. Look at your being in a different way. Look at what beautiful things you have within, and learn to recognize them.

I allow my body to relax... I breathe gently and deeply... My physical senses relax...

I can feel more and more how my body is calming down and relaxing... I direct my attention to within, as if I was looking through a window... I discover a silent space... tranquil... calm... Here I feel safe from any outside influence... I can feel the calm... the silence... My mind is quietening... it becomes silent and peaceful...

I experience the silence... a silence that calms the mind... the expansion of my thoughts fades... I concentrate on my true being... I am calmed... The lake of my mind is serene... clean... transparent... Everything is clear... I can feel my own presence... I feel the pure energy of my being... I am shining like a beautiful star of divine light... My original qualities begin to shine at the heart of my soul, like a fountain of water that comes from a spring... I begin to recognize these treasures that rise up within me...

I concentrate on them and make them emerge, feeling that I am those qualities...

I am a spiritual being... I am a being of light... I shine and sparkle with unlimited peace, happiness and love...

I feel the peace... I am at peace... I am a being of peace... I feel the love...

I am a being full of love... of good feelings, of acceptance towards everybody...

My heart is strong... I feel that I am a being without limitations... with great strength... I glimpse what I really am... a being of authentic light... strong... radiating this light towards all people... towards the whole world...

I stay in silence... and I smile.

Meditation 2
Waves of Light Run through your Body: an Experience of Incorporeal State

I feel comfortable... tranquil... I focus my eyes on a specific point and let them rest there... My hands are in my lap... I am aware of my breathing... I begin to breathe deeply, inhaling and exhaling... When I inhale, I imagine a light filling my lungs that relaxes me... it makes me serene... it calms me... On letting go of the air, I feel that all the tension, worries, confusion... are leaving me...

After some moments of deep breathing, I centre my attention on my feet, where I feel a gentle luminous energy... like a vibration that relaxes my feet... I mentally withdraw this energy that connects to my feet... I visualize how a white light goes slowly up my ankles... my legs... like a luminous current... I feel as if my feet, legs... were to disappear... become light... weightless... I carry on bringing my attention upwards, slowly through my body through   my   pelvis,   until   my   chest... I feel that current of warm light running through this part of my body...

Now I look at my hands... I separate them... I move my fingers... I relax them, feeling how that white light withdraws, going up my arms... My arms relax... my hands... my arms are weightless... This gentle luminous energy now goes up my neck and envelops my face... Waves of light and peace run over my face... the muscles of my face are relaxed... I feel very light... a pleasant feeling of wellbeing is filling all my being...

I experience a very deep peace within me... I concentrate this luminous energy at the centre of my forehead... I visualise this luminous energy as a star floating between my eyes... that radiates energy and light... I am live energy... I am light... my form is light... I am a being of light... I am free... different to my body... I feel incorporeal... beyond the awareness of my body...

I feel at peace... free... completely free of the limitations of this body and the physical world... I am a being of peace... I radiate this energy of peace in the form of vibrations that spread outwards... to the place I am in... to my surroundings... and all the atmosphere becomes peaceful and calm. I enjoy this state of being light.

Meditation 3. The Detached Observer

I am aware of the present moment and of time... The whole world is out there... I let go for a moment of what is happening around me... It is as if the world continued to turn, but I have stopped for a few minutes and turned into an observer... Mentally, I take a step back... I look around me as if I were in the inside of a room... the room of my mind... In this place, I can be with myself... at peace... calmed... free... Here I do not have pressures, or worries, or fears... Nothing and nobody can influence me... I can think... see things as they really are...

I am sitting like an observer, seeing through two windows... These windows are my eyes... I am not my eyes... I am aware of who is looking through these eyes... I am different to everything I am seeing...

I perceive that separation between the observer and the observed... I observe the things that surround me without judging, without analysing... I simply observe, remaining at peace with myself...

I see this world as a stage of a great unlimited theatre play... each human being is an actor playing their own role... I simply observe from my inner room... things come and go... nothing is permanent... I do not need to worry about anything or anybody...

I let things be... flow... I am at peace... calmed... I share this vibration of peace with all that surrounds me.

Meditation 4. Authentic Love

I sit in silence, letting my thoughts go away from the outer world... I allow my mind to relax... to calm down... I focus my attention on the heart of my being... My heart is like a sacred silent place where I can feel what I really am... I am peaceful and light... a loving being... strong... secure... kind...

I have many virtues and qualities that I can share with others... Now my attention is going towards the quality of love... I imagine love like a seed in my heart waiting to awaken... grow... and flower... like a rose... For this, I only have to accept... believe... feel... that I am a being of love... I am full of love... I am love...

Letting go of the past... letting go of expectations... fears... negative feelings... forgiving... opening my heart... feeling that it is cleansed and this energy of love is as pure as the clean water flowing from a waterfall. Nothing and nobody have touched it... this is a love that asks for nothing in exchange... the love of a clean heart is unselfish... free of egotism and expectations... It makes truth and sincerity grow... acceptance and understanding...

I open my heart completely to love... I inhale deeply... I visualise my heart expanding, filling itself with this energy of pure love... I exhale slowly... and I visualise radiating this light of love from the deepest part of my heart towards the world... I am a beautiful being of light radiating peace and love... I am love... I am full of love... I feel love... I love myself and accept myself...

Meditation 5. The Healing Power of Love

Experience of God as an energy that heals and cleans the self with its light, power and love.

I relax. I calm my mind and breathing.

I imagine a beautiful beam of white light coming out from the centre of my forehead... It leaves me and goes beyond this room towards space... I feel that I am floating... detached from my body and surroundings...My consciousness is transported in that beam of light towards a space without limits... beyond the sun, the moon and the stars... It is a dimension of infinite light, beyond time... where there is silence and absolute quietness.

I see myself floating in that ocean of light... In that ocean there are many different kinds of waves... waves that are not of water, but rather waves of light... Some waves carry peace... others love... others happiness... I bathe in these waves... I allow myself to be carried by these waves... I feel how my mind is filling up with so much light and strength... On the screen of my mind, I can visualise where those luminous waves come from...

In front of me there appears a Being of Light that is silent and strong like the sun in a clear sky... It is a benevolent light... sweet... and loving... There is nothing to be afraid of... It sends me rays of light that melt my fears and weaken my resistances... It is like a magnet that takes me towards the depth of that ocean of Light... I feel that my nature is light...

All the thoughts of the physical world disappear. Only this world is real... I feel a healing energy of love that penetrates my thoughts... It penetrates my feelings... I feel bathed by that love... revitalised by that love... Love... Power... Light... All these beautiful waves... intense... come to me from this Spiritual Sun that resides in that infinite space of silence...

Meditation 6. Free Yourself from Fear

Breathe deeply. You should say to yourself "relax, calm yourself", while you slowly let go of the air. Repeat until you are tranquil and centred.

Become serene and feel a sensation of peace and wellbeing. Maintain this serenity on breathing. Free yourself of worries on letting go of the air.

I sit comfortably like an observer in silence... I let go of everything around me... objects, people, responsibilities, places... I focus my mind on the present moment... I let the serenity... the tranquillity... envelop me... In this calm I can see the dark corners of my being... Like shadows, I can see the fears, anxieties, guilt, unhappiness, weaknesses, that lie hidden there... Fear has poisoned my being, it has stolen my peace, my happiness and my self-respect...

I accept that there is fear within me... I observe it and I realize that I am not that fear... I am not that weakness... it is not real, it is a shadow...

I focus now on what is real: it is love... it is peace... it is wellbeing... it is the purity of the soul, what is real, authentic and true... I only have to access these original qualities and allow these energies to heal and strengthen my soul... To do this, I continue to observe calmly... with patience... I do not allow my mind to judge, or analyse what is happening to me... everything that has happened to me forms part of the past... I have learned from my mistakes... I forgive myself... I forgive others...

I continue to go forward... I only observe feeling who I am... I am a being of light... a peaceful being... that radiates light like a small candle that lights up a dark room, and dissipates the darkness inside... Conscious of who I am... I imagine that I am in the presence of a benevolent Being of Light that emanates an infinite love, peace and happiness... It is a powerful ocean of love that can dissolve all my fears, the pain and suffering that there is inside my soul...

I open my heart... and mentally I say: "here are my fears... They are Yours... They are no longer useful to me... I hand them over to you... I absorb your light... I absorb your love and let it reach each dark corner of my being... I feel how your powerful light, full of love, touches my fears... they dissolve and I am freed... I let go of all worries... The weaknesses and problems no longer have power over me... I feel that God is with me... that He accepts me as I am... He comforts me... I feel safe... at peace... in an immense peace... and free of worries...".

I enjoy this present moment in His company and I share this peace and love with the world. I keep the divine presence in my being.

Meditation 7. Change a Habit

Decide on a habit that you want to change. For example, impatience. We will focus this meditation on changing impatience. You can apply it to other habits.

I relax and prepare to go inside towards my being.

I am aware of the unwanted habit of becoming impatient...

As I sit in meditation, I relax my body.

I become the observer of my own thoughts and feelings...

Affirming my true identity as soul, I remember my real nature is one of calmness, peace and power...

I focus on the power of peace, inviting it in and welcoming it into my thoughts and feelings from deep within.... enjoying the calm contentment which it brings...

On the screen of my mind, I begin to visualise patience...

I see myself in a situation where I normally become impatient ...

I now see myself as being completely full with the attribute of patience...

I shape my feelings around the idea and image of patience.... unhurried and relaxed... calm and watchful...

If necessary, I can wait... forever.... with patience

I am free of the desire for certain outcomes...

I see how I respond with patience...

I see the effect of my patience in others within the situation...

I now know how I will speak with patience, walk with patience and act patiently in the reality of the situation...

I recognize my inner peace of spirit as the mother of my newly created patient attitude...

I maintain this peace, which generates serenity and patience in my soul.

Meditation 8. The Power of Silence

To enter into the experience of silence is not to be blank of thoughts or with a feeling of inner emptiness. The silence is the silence of the mind in which the generation of wasteful thoughts has ceased and a feeling of quietness, serenity and harmony is generated. When the mind is calm and becomes peaceful, you develop the capacity to observe and separate yourself from the things that surround you and you see them from another perspective. Silence connects you to the power that can take you beyond any negative experience and strengthens you to enjoy a positive and full life.

* * *

Consider your mind as a stage, and each thought, feeling, emotion as a scene in the film of your life... Relax... Don't try to control anything... Observe how your thoughts pass through your mind... Don't identify with any of them... Only observe... Look where they take you... Observe what happens inside you... Do not judge... The thoughts flow through your mind as if they were clouds that are crossing the sky until everything is clear and open... The mind is becoming calm, making itself peaceful... like the surface of the sea when it is serene...

Now, be conscious of the sounds that are produced around you... Stay here and now as an observer who sees and feels every-thing from a point of calm and tranquillity, behind these eyes... Feel the calm... the tranquillity... that comes from within you... Look around you... Observe without interpreting or judging... Try to perceive the space that surrounds you...

Now centre your attention on a point of the room... If any other thought comes along to distract you... direct it gently towards that point as if it were to melt in it... Feel the silence that is created through the power of concentration. Consciously, create a positive, peaceful, elevated thought, that you repeat slowly in your mind, leaving a space of silence between one thought and another, while you keep the focus on that point...

I am a being of peace... I am at peace... I feel the peace... I am light... I am a being of light... My nature is of light... I am light... peace and silence... I am feeling the silence between one thought and the next... I feel only peace... I listen to the peace... a silent peace... calmed... full... This peace and silence attracts the ocean of peace... I feel the attraction towards my home of silence and peace... In this peace and silence, I strengthen myself... my mind rests in that calm and quietness...

I experience a light that fills me... it recharges me... it renews me... it heals me... it frees me... I am free... completely free... nothing of the past exists... now I am at peace... I leave my mind in silence, as if I were floating on a sea of peace for a few minutes...

Meditation 9. Enjoy and Radiate

You need to get back your inner power by elevating your awareness and connecting with God. In this way you can maintain the happiness, the peace that is within you and not be influenced by others or the atmosphere that surrounds you. That way you maintain your harmony. This gives you hope.

In this meditation, we are going to fill ourselves with spiritual power in order to be a beacon of light that sends the light of love and peace to the broken and hurt hearts of many human beings. A beacon of light that takes hope to the life of others.

* * *

Imagine that God is in front of you like an inexhaustible fountain of supreme energy, of light and spiritual power... Think about the qualities that most attract you... the ocean of peace... the ocean of love... the ocean of happiness... the ocean of forgiveness...

In the same way as you look at the Sun and feel its rays of light and heat on your face, let this spiritual Sun bathe you with its light... it fills you with spiritual power... it awakens your hidden potential... your original goodness... your greatness... You can feel the greatness of your being...

I am strong... I am brave... within me there is strength and an abundance of peace at my disposal... I am a strong soul full of spiritual power... This power helps me to maintain my happiness... to have hope... to deal with obstacles and difficult situations... I am discovering my authentic being of light... powerful... radiating this light that is so pure and peaceful...

I become a beacon of light... stable... calmed... generous... sharing the light of the love of God with others... the love that gives hope, trust... the love that protects and gives courage... I am an instrument to bring hope to this world... a light for the world that has good elevated feelings towards all the beings of this Earth... my heart overflows with love... with good desires towards all and they are spread like the fragrance of flowers... a fragrance that is given as a gift, freely... a fragrance of love that, with gentleness, soothes the suffering of others... it is a massage for the heart.

I am a being of peace... I am light... I am a beacon of light that glows in the dark... gives peace where peace is missing...

Stay some moments in silence in order to feel how these vibrations, so peaceful and pure, spread.

And, slowly, return to this present moment conscious of how you are, of your body and what surrounds you. Prepare yourself to carry on radiating peace, light and love out of action.

Meditation 10. Let Go of Pain

Open your heart and let the pain go. Learn to let go.

Relax your body and observe how your breathing calms down.

Relax your mind, make your thought slow down and your mind calm itself.

Let the energy of peace envelop your being and dissolve the tensions.

Your body relaxed, your mind serene.

Something hurts you in your heart. Observe it without judging it, without questioning it.

Let the energy of peace envelop that pain and dissolve it.

It forms part of the past.

Now I let it go. I let go of it.

I give myself up to peace.

The light of peaceful and serene love surrounds me in an energy that dissolves the pain.

I let the wings of my heart open without fear.

I am brave. I am strong. I trust.

I accept and I forgive.

My being wants to be free in order to enjoy this instant.

The pain has already gone. It does not belong to me any more.

I feel freed. Peace floods my being and my heart opens to love.

I am peace.

I am love.

Meditation 11. Discover Your Inner Mentor

Relax your body and allow yourself to be fully present, here, listening to the sounds around you, feeling what you are feeling.

Now send love to each part of your body: your feet, your buttocks, your lungs, your back, your shoulders, your face, your eyes, your nose, and thus send love to each part of your body until you feel it from your feet to your head.

Now you send love to each thought that appears on the screen of your mind, you visualise how your energy is concentrated on the inside of the centre of your forehead.

See the screen of your mind, and try to make each thought that you generate full of the energy of love that is slowly invading you.

Love what you yourself create: each thought.

The energy of love is present in each thought that appears in your mind.

That part of you that can give you love is your inner mentor. As you practise spending time with yourself in this way, you will find that your insecurity and your fears begin to disappear and new possibilities appear before you.

MEDITATION CREDITS:

José Andrés Ramírez Urcuyo helped in the elaboration of the commentaries of Meditations 1, 2, 3, 4, 5, 6, 8, 9.

Meditation 7 Change a Habit is from *In The Light of Meditation* by Mike George.

NOTES & REFERENCES

1. Salvador García's book on self-esteem: *Autoestima, estrés y trabajo*.

2. The *Mahabharat* is an enormous book of many volumes; one is the sacred text, *The Bhagavad Gita*, considered to be one of the oldest sacred books of India.

3. Anthony de Mello, *The Way to Love*.

4. Erich Fromm, *The Fear of Freedom*.

5. I was giving a talk in Malaga, in September 2005, when there was a plague of jellyfish and a vigorous attempt to control them.

6. "The lesser the trust, the more need for control." Salvador García, *Autoestima, estrés y trabajo*.

7. Anthony de Mello, *The Way to Love*.

8. *Sanskara*: a word in Sanskrit that refers to the habits, personality traits, impressions recorded on the register of our being, and that lead us to think and act in a certain way. There are healthy *sanskaras* and unhealthy *sanskaras*.

9. *"Today is beautiful."* Kayyam.

10. Scale of values. Pilar Quera and Miriam Subirana, *Valores para vivir. Manual para educadores I. (Values for Life. Instructors' Training Manual I)*

11. Rabindranath Tagore (1861-1941), known as Gurudev, was a Brahmin poet and philosopher, artist, playwright, novelist and composer who was awarded the Nobel Prize in Literature in 1913.

Born in Calcutta, he travelled the world as a cultural reformer and supporter of Mahatma Gandhi.

12. full of meaning. Pilar Quera and Miriam Subirana, *Valores para vivir.*

13. "It is easier to trust someone who has self-esteem". Salvador García, *Autoestima, estrés y trabajo.*

14. Ram Prakash, meditation teacher at Brahma Kumaris centre, New York. An Extract from Ima Sanchís' interview with Ram Prakash was published in "La Contra", *La Vanguardia*, 13th September, 2001.

15. "you will have finally understood what love is". Anthony de Mello, *The Way to Love.*

16. "intuition is the organ of direct knowledge..." Gottfried Purucker, *Studies in Occult Philosophy.*

17. Viktor Frankl *Man's Search for Meaning.*

18. See *Who Rules in Your Life?* by Miriam Subirana about the knowledge of how our mind and the energy of thought works.

BIBLIOGRAPHY

Nikki de Carteret: *Soul Power – The Transformation that Happens When you Know* (published by O Books, UK, 2003).

Paulo Coelho: *The Alchemist*. HarperCollins Publishers, New York, USA, 1993. (British edition: HarperCollins Publishers, London, 2002.

Simon L. Dolan, Salvador García, Miriam Díez Piñol: *Autoestima, estrés y trabajo (Self-esteem)* McGraw-Hill. Madrid, 2005.

Erich Fromm: *The Fear of Freedom*, (1941) Routledge, London, 2001.

Erich Fromm, *Escape from Freedom*. Henry Holt, New York, USA.

Carmen García Ribas, *Tengo miedo. Carisma y liderazgo a través de la gestión del propio miedo*. Ediciones Granica, Barcelona, 2003.

Mike George: *Discover Inner Peace*. Duncan Baird Publishers, London, UK, 1999.

Mike George: *Learn to Relax*. Duncan Baird Publishers, London, UK, 1997.

Mike George: *The 7 AHA!s of Highly Enlightened Souls*. John Hunt Publishers, UK, 2005.

Mike George: *In the Light of Meditation*. O Books, UK, 2004. New York, USA, EE UU.

Dadi Janki: *Inside Out*. BK Publications, London, 2003).

Pilar Jericó: *No Miedo. En la empresa y en la vida*. Alienta Editorial, Barcelona, 2003.

Krishnamurti, 2003: *On Freedom*. Harper Collins Publishers, New York, USA. British edition: *On Freedom*. Gollancz, London, 2006.

Harriet Lerner: *Fear and Other Uninvited Guests*. Harper Collins Publishers, New York, USA, 2004.

Niklas Luhmann: *Trust and Power*, John Wiley & Sons, Chichester, UK, 1979.

Anthony de Mello: *The Way to Love*. Image Book, Doubleday, New York, USA, 1995.

Raymond A. Moody: *Life After Life*. HarperCollins Publishers, New York, USA, 2001.

Ken O'Donnell: *La última frontera*. Asociación Brahma Kumaris. Barcelona, Spain 2006.

Judith Pemell: *The Soul Illuminated*. Lothian Books. Melbourne, Australia, 2003.

Margaret Pinkerton: *Moving on*. Eternity Ink. Sydney, Australia, 1996.

Oriol Pujol Borotau: *Nada por obligación, todo por ilusión*. Amat Editorial. Barcelona, 2004.

Gottfried Purucker: *Studies in Occult Philosophy*. Theosophical University Press. Passadena, 1973.

Anthony Strano: *Eastern Thought for the Western Mind*. BK Publications. London, 2006.

Miriam Subirana Vilanova, and Ramón Ribalta: *Who Rules in Your Life*. O Books. Winchester, UK, 2008. New York, USA.

Eckhart Tolle: *The Power of Now: A Guide to Spiritual Enlightenment*. New World Library. Novato. USA, 1999.

Raja Yoga Meditation Centres of the
Brahma Kumaris World Spiritual University

The more than 9000 meditation centres of the Brahma Kumaris Organisation in 100 countries offer courses in positive thinking, overcoming stress, self-esteem, Raja Yoga meditation and personal leadership.

The Brahma Kumaris World Spiritual University is an international organisation which works in all areas of society for a positive change. Created in 1937, at present it offers and actively participates in a wide range of educational programmes for the development of human and spiritual values.

For more information, visit the web page: www.bkwsu.org

INTERNATIONAL HEADQUARTERS

Post Box No 2
Mount Abu 307501, Rajasthan
India
T (+91) 2974 238261- 68
E abu@bkivv.org

INTERNATIONAL CO-ORDINATING OFFICE & REGIONAL OFFICE FOR EUROPE & THE MIDDLE EAST

Global Co-operation House
65-69 Pound Lane
London NW10 2HH
United Kingdom
T (+44) 20 8727 3350
E london@bkwsu.org

REGIONAL OFFICES

AFRICA
Brahma Kumaris Raja Yoga Centre
Global Museum, Maua Close,
Westlands, PO Box 123 - 00606
Nairobi
T (+254) 20-3743572 / 3741239
F 254-20-3743885
E nairobi@bkwsu.org

ASIA PACIFIC
78 Alt Street, Ashfield
Sydney NSW2131
Australia
T (+61) 2 9716 7066
E ashfield@au.bkwsu.org

THE AMERICAS & THE CARIBBEAN

Global Harmony House
46 S. Middle Neck Road
Great Neck, New York 11021
USA
T (+1) 516 773 0971
E newyork@bkwsu.org

RUSSIA, CIS & THE BALTIC COUNTRIES

2 Gospitalnaya Ploschad, Build. 1
Moscow 111020
Russia
T (+7) 495 263 02 47
F (+7) 495 261 32 24
E moscow@bkwsu.org

SPAIN
Main centre

Diputacio 329, Pral
Barcelona 08009
Spain
T (+34) 934 877 667
E barcelona@es.bkwsu.org

ABOUT THE AUTHOR

MIRIAM SUBIRANA VILANOVA

www.miriamsubirana.com

President of the World Spiritual Brahma Kumaris Association in Spain and PhD in Fine Arts, she trained at the Faculty of Fine Arts at the University of Barcelona and at the California College of Arts and Crafts of Oakland.

Miriam is an international speaker who combines leadership skills with the use of art and creative meditation techniques. As a public speaker, Miriam has given lectures to different audiences from over a thousand people to small selective groups in over 20 countries. She has motivated hundreds of people to transform their lives opening up to new possibilities that permit the realization of one's own potential.

She co-ordinates numerous programs, projects, seminars and retreats whose objective is to help towards knowing oneself, re-finding ones identity and enjoying a fuller life.

She has shown her art work in galleries and exhibition rooms in Spain, Portugal, France, Denmark, England, New York, São Paulo, Hong Kong, amongst other cities of the world.

She has co-ordinated the creation of two spiritual art galleries in Mount Abu and Agra (India).

Her book, *Who Rules in Your Life?* has been re-edited four times in three years (in Spanish), is called   The Spanish publication of *Dare to Live*, published in 2007, is already in its second edition. She also publishes articles on matters of personal development and has recorded many CDs with guided meditations.

"Miriam Subirana's brushstrokes, so full of spontaneous vitality and colour, show an aesthetic confidence in a new culture that affirms the possibilities of harmony between being, earth and cosmos. These canvases open us up to a spirituality that flows and gives you encouragement. In Miriam Subirana's landscapes there exists a thread of hope that delights and makes us brave."

José Ribas, writer.

BOOKS

O is a symbol of the world, of oneness and unity. In different cultures it also means the "eye," symbolizing knowledge and insight. We aim to publish books that are accessible, constructive and that challenge accepted opinion, both that of academia and the "moral majority."

Our books are available in all good English language bookstores worldwide. If you don't see the book on the shelves ask the bookstore to order it for you, quoting the ISBN number and title. Alternatively you can order online (all major online retail sites carry our titles) or contact the distributor in the relevant country, listed on the copyright page.

See our website **www.o-books.net** for a full list of over 500 titles, growing by 100 a year.

And tune in to myspiritradio.com for our book review radio show, hosted by June-Elleni Laine, where you can listen to the authors discussing their books.

SOME RECENT O BOOKS

In the Light of Meditation
Mike George

A classy book. A gentle yet satisfying pace and is beautifully illustrated. Complete with a CD of guided meditation commentaries, this is a true gem among meditation guides. **Brainwave**

1903816610 £11.99 $19.95

The Four Faces of Woman
Restoring Your Authentic Power, Recovering Your Eternal Beauty
Caroline T. Ward

I've always thought of Caroline Ward as a competitor - because more people would turn up for her retreats than mine. After reading "Four Faces of Woman" I can understand why. For any woman who believes she's on a spiritual journey, and wondering where it's leading, you won't find a better route-map than this. **Paul Wilson**, best selling author, *"The Calm Series"*

9781846940866 272pp £9.99 $19.95

7 Aha's of Highly Enlightened Souls
Mike George

A very profound, self empowering book. Each page bursting with wisdom and insight. One you will need to read and reread over and over again! **Paradigm Shift**

1903816319 128pp **£5.99 $11.95**

Don't Get MAD Get Wise
Why no one ever makes you angry!
Mike George

After "The Power of Now", I thought I would never find another self-help book that was even a quarter as useful as that. I was wrong. Mike George's book on anger, like a Zen master's teaching, is simple yet profound. This isn't one of those wishy-washy books about forgiving people. It's just the opposite....a spiritually powerful little book. **Marian Van Eyk**, *Living Now Magazine*

1905047827 160pp **£7.99 $14.95**

A Global Guide to Interfaith
Reflections From Around the World
Sandy Bharat

This amazing book gives a wonderful picture of the variety and excitement of this journey of discovery. **Rev Dr. Marcus Braybrooke**, President of the World Congress of Faiths

1905047975 336pp **£19.99 $34.95**

A Pagan Testament
The literary heritage of the world's oldest new religion
Brendan Myers

A remarkable resource for anyone following the Wicca/Pagan path. It gives an insight equally into wiccan philosophy, as well as history and practise. We highly recommend it. A useful book for the individual witch; but an essential book on any covens bookshelf. **Janet Farrar** and **Gavin Bone**, authors of *A Witches Bible, The Witches Goddess, Progressive Witchcraft*

9781846941290 384pp **£11.99 $24.95**

Everyday Buddha
Lawrence Ellyard

Whether you already have a copy of the Dhammapada or not, I recommend you get this. If you are new to Buddhism this is a great place to start. The whole feel of the book is lovely, the layout of the verses is clear and the simple illustrations are very beautiful, catching a feel for the original work. His Holiness the Dalai Lama's foreword is particularly beautiful, worth the purchase price alone. Lawrence's introduction is clear and simple and sets the context for what follows without getting bogged down in information... I congradulate all involved in this project and have put the book on my recommended list. **Nova Magazine**

1905047304 144pp **£9.99 $19.95**

Helena's Voyage
A mystic adventure
Paul Harbridge

A beautiful little book, utterly charming in its simplicity. **Rabbi Harold Kushner,** author of *"When Bad Things Happen to Good People"*

9781846941146 48pp **£9.99 $19.95**

Living With Honour
A Pagan Ethics
Emma Restall Orr

This is an excellent pioneering work, erudite, courageous and imaginative, that provides a new kind of ethics, linked to a newly appeared complex of religions, which are founded on some very old human truths. **Professor Ronald Hutton,** world expert on paganism and author of *The Triumph of the Moon*

9781846940941 368pp **£11.99 $24.95**

Peace Prayers
From the World's Faiths
Roger Grainger

Deeply humbling. This is a precious little book for those interested in building bridges and doing something practical about peace. **Odyssey**

1905047665 144pp **£11.99 $19.95**

Shamanic Reiki
Expanded Ways of Workling with Universal Life Force Energy
Llyn Roberts and Robert Levy

The alchemy of shamanism and Reiki is nothing less than pure gold in the hands of Llyn Roberts and Robert Levy. Shamanic Reiki brings the concept of energy healing to a whole new level. More than a how-to-book, it speaks to the health of the human spirit, a journey we must all complete. **Brian Luke Seaward**, Ph.D., author of *Stand Like Mountain, Flow Like Water, Quiet Mind, Fearless Heart*

9781846940378 208pp £9.99 $19.95

The Good Remembering
A Message for our Times
Llyn Roberts

Llyn's work changed my life. "The Good Remembering" is the most important book I've ever read. **John Perkins**, *NY Times* best selling author of *Confessions of an Economic Hit Man*

1846940389 96pp £7.99 $16.95

The Last of the Shor Shamans
Alexander and Luba Arbachakov

The publication of Alexander and Luba Arbachakov's 2004 study of Shamanism in their own community in Siberia is an important addition to the study of the anthropology and sociology of the peoples of Russia. Joanna Dobson's excellent English translation of the Arbachakov's work brings to a wider international audience a fascinating glimpse into the rapidly disappearing traditional world of the Shor Mountain people. That the few and very elderly Shortsi Shamans were willing to share their beliefs and experiences with the Arbachakov's has enabled us all to peer into this mysterious and mystic world. **Frederick Lundahl**, retired American Diplomat and specialist on Central Asia

9781846941276 96pp **£9.99 $19.95**

Thoughtful Guide to God
Howard Jones

As thoughtful as the title claims, this is thorough, with excellent background, history and depth, and is just right for the kind of person who sees, feels and perhaps has already begun to find the fusion of consciousness that shows the way out of the confusion of our times towards a way of being that is positive, without being naive, and profoundly informative, without being pedantic. If you have a brain, heart and soul, and the interest to see where they become one, this book is a must. **Odyssey**

1905047703 400pp **£19.99 $39.95**

The Thoughtful Guide to Religion
Why it began, how it works, and where it's going
Ivor Morrish

A massive amount of material, clearly written, readable and never dry. the fruit of a lifetime's study, a splendid book. It is a major achievement to cover so much background in a volume compact enough to read on the bus. Morris is particularly good on illustrating the inter-relationships betwen religions. I found it hard to put down. **Faith and Freedom**

190504769X 384pp **£24.99 $34.95**

Gospel of Falling Down
The beauty of failure, in an age of success
Mark Townsend

It's amazing just how far I was drawn into Mark's words. This wasn't just a book but an experience. I never realized that failure could be a creative process. Editor, *Voila Magazine*

1846940095 144pp £9.99 $16.95

How to Meet Yourself
...and find true happiness
Dennis Waite

An insightful overview of the great questions of life itself: a compelling inner tapestry that encourages the reader to willingly embrace life being exactly as it is. Readable, relevant and recommended. **Chuck Hillig,** author of *Enlightenment for Beginners*

1846940419 360pp £11.99 $24.95

Love, Healing and Happiness
Spiritual wisdom for secular times
Larry Culliford

This will become a classic book on spirituality...immensely practical and grounded. A nourishing book that lays the foundation for a higher understanding of human suffering and hope. **Reinhard Kowalski,** Consultant Clinical Psychologist and author of *The Only Way Out Is In*

1905047916 224pp £10.99 $19.95

Ordinary Secrets
Notes for your spiritual journey
Robert Y. Southard

*Turned off by lofty teachers, levitating gurus, and approaches to spiritu-
ality that require years of training? Want to start today to live a more
productive, relaxed, ecstatic life? If so, this is your book. In it Bob
Southard shares his ordinary secrets that will send you on your way to an
extraordinary life.* **John Perkins**, New York Times Best Selling author
of Confessions of An Economic Hit Man

9781846940675 96pp **£7.99 $16.95**

The 9 Dimensions of the Soul
Essence and the Enneagram
David Hey

*David Hey has taken the psychological elements of the Enneagram &
added them to the study of Essence, which are the qualities of being. It
makes for an in-depth and enlightening analysis. He even delves into how
countries and hierarchies function under the rules of the Enneagram. For
those wanting to learn more about themselves from the core levels to the
displayed traits, this is the book for you!* **Rev Dr Sandra Gaskin**, www.
spirit-works.net

1846940028 160pp **£10.99 $19.95**

The Barefoot Indian
The Making of a Messiahress
Julia Heywood

The book is warm, funny, but altogether life changing. It teaches lessons that are infinitely valuable, on life itself and the nature of the cosmos and the ailments of the human race. They are so many answers, and my old self is itching to show off and tell you some, but I am not able to. The book is one you must journey through and reflect upon by yourself. A touching and life changing read, "The Barefoot Indian" is definitely one to pick up the next time you visit your local bookstore. It is an easy and essential read for all ages. She Unlimited Magazine

1846940400 112pp £7.99 $16.95

Palmistry: From Apprentice to Pro in 24 Hours
The Easiest Palmistry Course Ever Written
Johnny Fincham

Inspiring, life changing. Daily Express

9781846940477 240pp £9.99 $16.95

The Four Faces of Woman
Restoring Your Authentic Power, Recovering Your Eternal Beauty
Caroline T. Ward

I've always thought of Caroline Ward as a competitor - because more people would turn up for her retreats than mine. After reading "Four Faces of Woman" I can understand why. For any woman who believes she's on a spiritual journey, and wondering where it's leading, you won't find a better route-map than this. **Paul Wilson**, best selling author, *The Calm Series*

9781846940866 272pp **£9.99 $19.95**

The Good Remembering
A Message for our Times
Llyn Roberts

Llyn's work changed my life. "The Good Remembering" is the most important book I've ever read. **John Perkins**, *NY Times* best selling author of *Confessions of an Economic Hit Man*

1846940389 96pp **£7.99 $16.95**

The Message
Your Secrets in the Cards
Deborah Leigh

This book is an eye opener to everyone who reads it, as well as a message telling us it is time we began controlling our own destiny. It will open your eyes to your choices in life, and how each path you choose may lead to a different destination. You don't have to be a lawyer to understand it, nor do you have to have psychic abilities. I give it five stars and also give it to my friends and family members as gifts! **Sherry Jessop**, author of *The Great BooDinie Bird* books, *Faith* and *The Capture, Heart & Soul* poetry

9781846940958 272pp **£11.99 $24.95**

The Secret of Home
homesouls Guide to Abundant Living
Lindsay Halton

Architect Lindsay Halton has produced an imaginative, transformative and alchemical work. Physical aspects of our homes are much deeper reflections of our spiritual lives and paths. "The Secret of Home" will enable us to view our home through the theatre of our Soul, to reassess our life's journey and consider our choices in profound and perhaps novel ways. **Dr. Sandra Goodman**, Ph.D. Editor and Director of Positive Health

9781846940903 288pp £11.99 $24.95

Unlock Your Psychic Powers
Richard Lawrence

Explains clearly every aspect of seeing the future... and how to awaken your own psychic abilities. **Daily Mail**

9781846940880 208pp £9.99 $19.95

The House of Wisdom
Yoga of the East and West
Swami Dharmananda Saraswati and Santoshan

Swamiji has shared her wisdom with her students for many years. Now her profound and enlightening writings, and those of Santoshan, are made available to a wider audience in this excellent book. The House of Wisdom is a real treasure-house of spiritual knowledge. **Priya Shakti** (Julie Friedeberger), author of *The Healing Power of Yoga*

1846940249 224pp £11.99 $22.95